T0304524

THE

100

FORMULA

THE 100X FORMULA

How to Win in Investing, Life and Relationships

FORMULA

SIDDHARTHA RASTOGI AND KOUSHIK MOHAN

PENGUIN
BUSINESS

An imprint of Penguin Random House

PENGUIN BUSINESS

Penguin Business is an imprint of the Penguin Random House group of companies whose addresses can be found at global.penguinrandomhouse.com

Published by Penguin Random House India Pvt. Ltd
4th Floor, Capital Tower 1, MG Road,
Gurugram 122 002, Haryana, India

First published in Penguin Business by Penguin Random House India 2024

ISBN 9780143463566

Typeset in Sabon LT Std by MAP Systems, Bengaluru, India
Printed at Thomson Press India Ltd, New Delhi

www.penguin.co.in

Disclaimer

The content of this book and the ideas expressed therein solely belong to the authors. The information provided should not be treated as recommendations for trading and investing in financial instruments. Some of the stocks mentioned may be held by the authors and/or their employers but are not recommendations for trading and investing. Readers should conduct thorough research before acting on any information presented as market data is subject to change and its accuracy cannot be guaranteed. This book is for informational purposes only and does not constitute a solicitation for financial transactions. Reproduction of confidential information is prohibited without the authors' consent. The opinions, figures and data included in the book are subject to change without notice. The authors make no warranties regarding the accuracy of the information presented, and readers are encouraged to verify facts independently. As past performance does not guarantee future results, future performance based on the formulas discussed is not guaranteed. The authors are not liable for losses resulting from investment decisions made based on the book.

Contents

Foreword

At the outset, I take this opportunity to congratulate authors Siddhartha Rastogi and Koushik Mohan for penning down *The 100X Formula*. This book divulges the secrets to living life with purpose and I commend the authors for their passion and wonderful presentation of ideas.

Life is an intricate journey in which our decisions are intertwined with our destiny, in a deeper quest to find the purpose of one's being within the larger universe. This journey has its moments of difficulties, victories and an incessant search for excellence. The authors profoundly invite readers to transcend the limits of the usual paths to success through this book, which covers investing, relationships, entrepreneurship and what it means to be working in a corporate structure.

This book is essentially a blend of storytelling, ancient wisdom and modern research. The authors have attempted to demystify the secrets behind success, which will help readers overcome life's trials resiliently, in a purposeful direction. The book exhorts people to do more than they usually do, stretch beyond their boundaries and get exceptional results out of their efforts.

The authors, Siddhartha and Koushik, with their unique blend of narrative flair and analytical acumen, subtly explain intricate ideas, making them accessible to readers from all walks of life. The narrative is woven around the journey of the protagonist, a girl who rises from rags to riches and finds solace in the timeless principles of Sanatan Dharma. Her story becomes a metaphor for the universal struggle and triumph that every individual encounters in life. The authors use this narrative not only to engage the readers but also to illustrate how ancient wisdom seamlessly integrates into our modern lives, providing a foundation for ethical decision-making and enduring success.

In a world that often feels like a roller-coaster ride, this book serves as a steady compass, guiding readers through the ups and downs with clarity. It is a must-read for anyone who aspires to succeed in life, investing and relationships, and goes beyond the conventional self-help genre, offering a deep exploration of the interconnectedness between individual choices and the grand design of the universe.

I wish the authors great success in all their endeavours.

Nitin Gadkari
Minister of Road Transport and Highways,
Government of India

A Note from Vasanth Kamath

Founder and CEO, smallcase

Siddhartha and Koushik are two of the sharpest minds in the world of finance. I was pleasantly surprised and delighted when Siddhartha called me on a Friday night and requested me to write a foreword to this book. As someone who has witnessed the dedication and ingenuity of Siddhartha and Koushik, I can attest to the authenticity and effectiveness of their wealth management principles.

In *The 100X Formula*, Siddhartha and Koushik take readers through the complexities of life, finance, investing and entrepreneurship, offering a road map to success. Drawing from their experiences and learnings, they present a refreshingly simple yet profoundly effective approach to achieving financial stability and personal growth. Their commitment to helping others achieve financial freedom shines through every page of this book, providing readers with not just theoretical concepts but also actionable insights grounded in real-life scenarios.

At the heart of their philosophy lies the recognition that, while predicting the future may be daunting, learning from the experiences of others and embracing simplicity can pave the way for success. Through their meticulously crafted narrative and the compelling story of Priya, readers are inspired to embark on a transformative journey—one that transcends mere financial gains and delves into the essence of a fulfilled life.

Whether you're grappling with financial uncertainty or simply seeking to optimize your investment strategy, *The 100X Formula* is an invaluable resource that promises to empower and enlighten you. Through its blend of practical advice, relatable anecdotes and timeless wisdom, this book has the power to transform not just your portfolio but your entire outlook on life.

In an era where financial literacy is paramount, Siddhartha and Koushik's work offers much-needed clarity. By distilling their insights into actionable strategies, they equip readers with the tools to build a secure future while pursuing their dreams.

May this book spark your curiosity and embolden you to embark on your financial journey. As you delve into these pages, may you uncover practical wisdom for managing your wealth, achieving financial freedom, personal growth and realizing your most cherished dreams.

Bengaluru
7 March 2024

1

The Paradox Called Life

Expectation and Hope

'I'd heard big cities had a lot to offer, so I packed my bags, left home and came to Delhi with dreams in my eyes. I convinced my mother that this was the only way to move forward in life and to guarantee a better future for my two little brothers. But six months in this city and I'm already losing my mind. This is not how I imagined things would turn out,' says Priya, an ambitious twenty-year-old girl, determined to provide for her family as the oldest sibling.

Priya's father died when she was only ten years old. Since then, her mother began working as a house help. Priya's mother is her role model—the plucky young woman is proud of her and desires to be as courageous as her. A fearless attitude, a dedication to hard work and the ability to face hardships is what her mother packed for her Delhi journey.

Like any woman trying to make her way in the world under her own steam, Priya was afraid that if she'd be unable to achieve anything within a few years, her relatives would either pressure her mother to get Priya married, or wash their hands off any responsibility towards her. She had imagined that life would change once she moved to a place like Delhi, but the reality isn't always sweet.

Power of Imagination or Waste of Time?

Don't you like to think of scenarios that make you feel happy, fulfilled, accomplished or proud?

Most of us like to daydream about things we don't have or are unlikely to have—owning a big house, a car, a healthy relationship, fame, power, love, strength, beauty, etc. The mere idea of having any of these makes us happy and we want to continue dreaming about them because it's easier that way. Daydreaming makes us feel like we are close to having achieved something which, in reality, is far, far away.

Imagination is a powerful thing. You can have everything you want, with none of the hard work involved in acquiring it. However, the easy pleasure that you get from a trip to la-la land is ephemeral. It ends, and you go back to your routine life. So it's advisable that you avoid wandering down this abyss, because you'll only be wasting your precious time.

> YOU HAVE ONE LIFE, CHASE YOUR DREAMS, FOLLOW YOUR HEART. COMFORT COMES FROM COMPLACENCY; THE DISCOMFORT OF STEPPING UP OR STEPPING OUT COMES FROM INNER FEAR. COMFORT ELIMINATES POTENTIAL; DISCOMFORT EXPANDS POSSIBILITIES.

Priya took the first step towards making that daydream a reality. **She knew that fantasizing wouldn't get her anywhere, and that it was high time she started acting to turn her dreams into reality.** She got a job as an office girl and was offered a salary of Rs 11,000 per month with the promise of a raise after a month, which never happened.

Reality Check

Priya lived alone in rented accommodation, for which she paid Rs 5000 per month. After deducting the bare minimum for food and other necessities from her salary, she was able to send the remaining money to her family, who lived on the outskirts of Karnataka. Being alone in the city with no contacts or acquaintances, Priya desperately needed a friend, someone she could talk to and share her highs and lows with. Soon, she did meet someone—a girl like her who was poor and was working as a waitress. Priya offered to stay with her in her rented PG (paying guest) accommodation. The girl agreed and soon, they started living together. After some time, Priya got her first salary which, instead of being electronically transferred to her bank account, was paid to her in cash. The girl stole those Rs 11,000 and ran away. She told Priya that she was going to meet her parents back in Kolkata and would be back soon, but she never returned. Priya kept calling her, but found that the girl had blocked her. Priya had no means of contacting her. The girl hadn't even paid her share of the rent.

With no salary in hand, Priya was shattered. She couldn't ask her mother for money. Even if she did, it wouldn't help—she knew this. This is when the first harsh dose of reality hit her. She was angry at herself and wanted to punish herself for trusting someone blindly.

But that, of course, wouldn't change anything either.

So, what could she do?

What now? That was the question that she kept asking herself that night.

Life Is Suffering

> DEEDS AND THEIR OUTCOMES ARE CYCLICAL. ONE UNDERGOES SUFFERING IN THE WORLD TO PAY FOR THEIR ILL DEEDS, WHETHER COMMITTED KNOWINGLY OR UNKNOWINGLY. ONE HAS TO PAY, IF NOT IN THIS WORLD, THEN IN THE OTHER WORLD.

The first thing Priya needed to realize was that life is difficult. In Buddhism, there are four noble truths. The first noble truth is '*Life is suffering*', or *Dukkha*. This tenet upholds that all of a person's experiences in life result in suffering and that they are unable to prevent this.

People might seek a temporary reprieve from their misery by engaging in enjoyable activities. However, the pain might return when the enjoyment ends, albeit it does not persist indefinitely. Acknowledging that there is pain is the first step towards ending it.

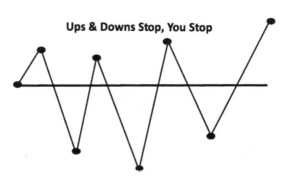

Ups & Downs Stop, You Stop

You in Your Life

As long as there are ups and downs in life, you are alive

Acceptance Is the First Step Towards a Solution

Acceptance helps minimize the enormity of your problems. But acceptance isn't achieved overnight. Before you accept things for the way they are, you cry about your problems. You moan about what you don't have and what you have always wanted to have.

But does that help? It doesn't.

Then why do we waste our time on self-pity?

That's because self-pity is easy, while the other option, where you have to go beyond the limits of your ability to solve your life's problems or achieve your goals, requires you to shed blood, sweat and tears.

> ACCEPTANCE SHIFTS THE FOCUS FROM THE PROBLEM TO THE SOLUTION.

Priya chose the second option. She could have left for her village after her roommate stole her earnings and she was left with no money in hand. Had she done that, her life would have gone back to square one. But she stayed. She accepted things for what they were and started looking for ways to achieve what she had come this far for.

However, not everyone chooses the latter. Why? Because they're scared. It's always the ugly incidents that are harder to forget than the beautiful ones. These unpleasant memories create prejudices, biases and, most detrimental of all, fear. Fear shouldn't be avoided—you should learn from it. And to do so, you'll first have to gain control of it.

> FIRST, A THOUGHT EMERGES IN THE MIND, THEN IT TURNS INTO INTENT. AND FINALLY, IT TAKES THE SHAPE OF REALITY.

The Need to Overcome Fear

Fear can be both a motivator and a deterrent. **People are more afraid of adverse consequences than they are of the process that one must follow to change the current circumstance.** They doubt the process, fearing that it may lead them on the wrong path or towards the wrong outcome. They fear bearing the cost of lost opportunity or losing everything in an ill-advised gamble.

They are filled with thoughts such as, 'What if it doesn't turn out to the way I want it?'

'What if I am wasting time?'

'What if I should be working on something else instead?'

'What if I get nothing in the end?'

'What if I get tainted?'

'What if I fail, and my family has to face the consequences?'

'What will society say?'

'What if I lose everything that I have?'

These 'what ifs' make you question your capabilities.

So how do you get rid of the fear?

The answer is: **You Don't.**

The idea is not to eradicate the feeling of fear. Fear is inescapable. The aim is to develop enormous courage. Courage doesn't mean the absence of fear; it means moving past the resistance engendered by fear. Courage helps you get started. As author Stephen King says of writing:

> FEAR PROVOKES THE FIRST TANGIBLE STEP. IT IS THE FIRST EMOTION THAT WILL LEAD TO ULTIMATE SUCCESS.

'The scariest moment is always just before you start. After that, things can only get better.'

Once you start something, you gradually begin to develop confidence. This is what the process looks like:

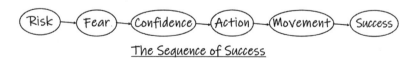

Risk — Fear — Confidence — Action — Movement — Success

The Sequence of Success

However, between courage and confidence, don't forget about the failures that will come your way. These failures will likely force you to take a step back and seek validation from others. You will want others to believe in you and to affirm that the path you have chosen is correct.

But what if you don't get any external validation?

In that case, you will probably complain about your problems and fall back to square one. The only alternative is to find, from the remotest corner of your heart and brain, the courage to proceed and to remember instances of the past when unexpected challenges were conquered—that will give you the confidence to act and move ahead.

Priya had no shoulder to cry on. Talking to her family would have made the situation worse as they would have simply called her back home. She cried all night. Many times, the thought of ending her life crossed her mind. After all, the new city wasn't treating her well. After that incident, she couldn't trust people any more. All she had was hope and a faint but burgeoning belief that things would eventually fall into place. *The only person she had was herself* and for the time being, that realization was enough. She knew that she didn't have the privilege or luxury to mope about.

She pondered what someone should ideally do in her situation. If you want to achieve something, you start working towards it. You face a few problems initially, but then you find ways to overcome them by pushing yourself, becoming more disciplined. Finally, you gain confidence when you achieve small wins. These small wins provide you

FEAR IS BETTER THAN REGRET. FEAR ARISES WHEN ONE TRIES, REGRET OCCURS WHEN ONE GIVES UP. WHICH ONE WILL YOU CHOOSE?

with further confidence, this new-found confidence prompts you to take bolder and bigger steps and, as a result, goals and targets are achieved.

At this point, Priya's primary problem was that she was underpaid. She was getting Rs 11,000 per month, of which she was spending Rs 5000 on rent, Rs 2000 on food and sending the rest to her family. She had no savings. So, she decided to do multiple jobs. She started working as a cook, earning Rs 2000 per house per month.

> MONEY IS ESSENTIAL, CRITICAL AND CRUCIAL. HAVING NONE HAS MORE SERIOUS REPERCUSSIONS THAN HAVING LOTS OF IT.

Within a month, she was able to get a cook's job at three houses. Now, her total income came to around Rs 17,000 per month. The goal was to make it Rs 20,000 per month. Priya acted to solve her problems and it worked out for her. She was exhausted from working fourteen hours a day, but at the end of the day, when she went to sleep, she didn't have to worry about her problems as she knew that the process, and her faith in the process, would enable her to overcome all her challenges soon.

Unlike Priya, most of us are not this wise, and even if we are, we don't act with similar wisdom and courage. **Most of the time, we get stuck because of one of two hindrances: *risk and fear.***

The fear of the effort (and the resultant pain) involved in solving the problems in our lives makes us want to avoid them. We ignore them, we pretend as if they don't exist, we accept them as our fate and hope that they will go away on their own, all the while daydreaming of a life without them, stuck in the abyss of reverie forever.

This in itself is a problem, so how does one solve it?

Even when one decides to take action, one is filled with uncertainty, a fear of what the opportunity will cost and apprehension about the 'what ifs' mentioned earlier, and one aborts all action.

To understand the solution, one first needs to understand how individuals perceive problems in their lives. Everybody has problems, but what is insurmountable to one might be a trivial hiccup to another.

Types of People

To analyse the different problems that we face in our lives, it is essential to first categorize people on the basis of the economic stratum they belong to:

1. **The rich:** They're the ones who don't seem to have any problems in their lives. This category can be further divided into two subcategories: those born with a silver spoon in their mouths and those who've burnt both ends of the candle to earn that silver spoon.

   The first subcategory is likely to have problems revolving around relationships, specifically with their parents, friends, peers, colleagues, juniors and other members of society and family who may be more successful or moneyed, as they always tend to compare. Such people are always running a race that never ends. Each desire becomes a need and the need forces them to compete with others constantly.

   The second subcategory of people often see their parents working hard to ensure their comfort and a secure future for their children. They generally don't have enough time for their children as they are busy pursuing financial goals; the children are mostly on their own and relationships can often get strained.

Those born with a silver spoon are sometimes the most carefree. However, everyone deals with some sort of problem or issue in their lives, even if the enormity and the nature of these problems vary.

What is visible to the eye is wealth, but the emotional and mental struggle behind the riches is seldom seen. Rich people are more likely to question their existence, their purpose or their path than someone whose first concern is to earn enough to survive the day.

Their thought process is: I have all this money, but what do I do with my life?

They start searching for meaning in their lives. They are in search of the happiness that emanates from healthy relationships. This may not seem unachievable, but the search can be exhausting. For some, this chase turns into substance abuse, a cycle that starts with peer pressure, moves to 'fun' and deteriorates into a desperate hunt for happiness.

2. <u>The middle class</u>: The second category desires stability. The majority of the middle class is worried only about getting stable jobs, getting into good colleges, saving up for retirement, a house, a dream car, etc.

    Their thought process is pretty structured—a good education will get them a high-paying, stable job which will help them meet their monetary goals. For them, the only ways to become rich and meet their targets are education and savings.

They also want to improve their social status and desire to have everything that the first category has. They want to have 'enough' money so that they can get where the 1 per cent are, and not just enough to make ends meet. For them, the struggle is making decisions related to saving and investing, and how to break the glass ceiling of the corporate rollercoaster.

3. <u>**The poor:**</u> They have only one problem—or so they think—and that's money. For them, issues related to relationships, temperaments and jealousy, all emanate from poverty, and all the problems in the world can be solved with money.

They are stuck in the vicious cycle of this belief. Having less money leads to anxiety, and to get rid of that anxiety, they use superficial distractions like alcohol, which further aggravate the problem.

They barely think of what they're going to do with their lives because their minds are already preoccupied with the immediate challenge of earning enough just to ensure survival.

Their first desire is not to get a car, but to earn enough so that they can meet their basic human needs. They want to have just enough money for the bare minimum: food, shelter, water, clothing and sleep.

The rich have abundance, the middle class have enough and desire abundance and the poor hope for enough, so it is true that life is easier if one has money, because in the end, humans are wired to survive, and without money, survival becomes a challenge.

Now that we know the general problems humans of every socio-economic stratum face, let's also understand the emergence of these problems.

How Do These Problems Become Problems?

The Buddha advocated for understanding the root of one's suffering to get past it. According to the Buddha, craving or desiring things is what leads to the majority of suffering. A person might crave something nice to eat or desire to go on a nice holiday or earn lots of money. The Buddha said that humans suffer because they are unhappy with their present existence and thus experience material cravings. This is the second noble truth, or *samudaya* (cause of grief).

Let's start from the very beginning, from the time you are born. When you enter this world, you're nothing but a human that breathes and exists. Remember, you're not a person, you don't have an identity. When you come into this world, you are untouched by any biases, opinions or emotional reactions.

However, as soon as you grow up and interact with other fully rational, healthy, functioning adult humans, are exposed to society and gain diverse experiences, you move beyond the state of just existing by attaining a personality.

Now that you have started acknowledging your identity, you're not just a human any more, but a person who listens to their consciousness, who takes actions not just to eat, sleep and breathe, but also to improve themself—a person who has a purpose or goals to fulfil.

The journey from becoming a human to a person is filled with experiences. These experiences shape your personality, but this personality never remains static. It evolves with every new experience you gain.

And with every experience, your opinions change too. A rigid opinion that you may have had in your twenties might not remain the same during your thirties. The reasons are experience and exposure; they are likely to change the way you look at certain aspects of life. One of the experiences that you may go through while growing up is realizing the scarcity of certain things in your life. The deprivations, however, will be different for every human being, depending, among other things, on which of the three categories of people (discussed earlier) they fall in.

> THOUGHTS LEAD TO INTENT, INTENT LEADS TO ACTIONS, ACTIONS LEAD TO EXPERIENCE AND EXPERIENCES MAKE ONE WISER AND PROPEL ONE FORWARD.

For instance, some children are born with silver spoons, but they don't have their parents around when they need them most. While some children have loving parents, but their parents don't have enough money to feed or support them. Some children feel their parents are not respected enough, and thus feel powerless. There is always something another person has that you desire, and something that you have that the other person has always wanted. Not having enough of something during your childhood makes you crave those things desperately later in life.

What will a child who has always lived in a rented house desire the most?

The answer is obvious: a house.

What will a child who was never appreciated by their parents while growing up seek?

External validation.

What will a child who was never truly recognized for their efforts feel the constant need to do?

Try to prove themselves each time.

You see, everything stems from scarcity and deprivation

Whenever you're deprived of something, you will always run after that thing, even if the process is tiring and may sometimes lead you nowhere. Your rich friend might want to spend time with their family, another friend might want to get into a reputed college so that they can get the kind of highly respected job that their parents never had, and the third friend might want a small house where they can live comfortably and get sound sleep.

> DEPRIVATION IS THE MOTHER OF SUCCESS. ABUNDANCE BRINGS ARROGANCE.

Is getting rid of deprivation the end to all suffering?

No.

Humans will always feel the scarcity of some or the other thing in their lives. They can never be truly satisfied.

So how does one overcome this suffering?

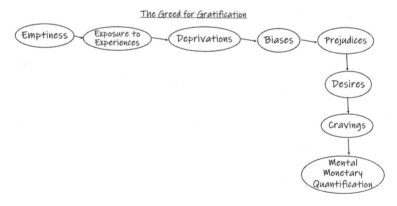

The Greed for Gratification

End to All Suffering

Now that you've understood the cause of suffering, the next thing is to learn that there is an end to suffering. This is the third noble truth, or *nirodha* (cessation).

The problems of each category of people that we have discussed above can end when they stop craving things. This is easier said than done. However, once you have the cure for these cravings, your suffering will come to an end.

Is money the solution to all problems?

If we look at the problems mentioned above, we can see the common thread in all three cases is money: the rich person who's deprived of parental love may overcome this problem if their parents, who are busy working day and night for money, start making their money work for them.

The other friend who wants that highly reputed job can only get one if they have enough to pay for their education. The third person, who needs a house to live in, is deprived of money. So, whether the dots are connected directly or indirectly, in the end, they lead to one thing, and that's money.

This is not to say that money is the solution to all problems, or that it's the only resource that can help one emerge from scarcity, but *it is definitely one of many solutions that can solve 99 per cent of your problems.*

A child doesn't realize the importance of money during childhood, but as soon as they grow up, all the problems that they have experienced seem to have only one solution—money.

Even problems that have nothing to do with finance turn out to have money at the root. For instance, if you have never found the love of your life, it's highly unlikely that someone will just bump into you one day and sparks will fly; obviously, life is not a movie. If you want a soulmate, a life partner, a better half, you'll have to go out there and explore. You may meet him or her in school, college, office, a social club, a hobby class or while travelling, and being at these places requires you to have money.

Some of the other problems, if not directly, are indirectly connected to money. That's the reason why every person, whether in the top 1 per cent or the remaining 99, needs to understand money.

Priya doesn't yet understand money. At this point, all she has in her mind is the craving to earn as much as she can from wherever she can. She's willing to work multiple jobs at times, just to make enough for herself and her family. But is there a better way for her to get what she wants? We'll figure out in the following chapters of this book.

This book is focused primarily on the 99 per cent of people who either don't have enough money or who are not successful with their money. One can make as much money as one wants—there is no upper threshold for money—but there is a lower threshold or a minimum. This book will teach you how to go past the lower threshold to achieve higher economic goals (including recognition, social status, corporate success, entrepreneurial prowess, etc.).

The fourth noble truth that Buddhism talks about is known as *magga* (path), which offers solutions to problems. In this book, we won't be discussing the Eightfold Path, which consists of eight steps Buddhists can follow to end suffering.

The Noble Eightfold Path

- Right understanding (*Samma ditthi*)
- Right thought (*Samma sankappa*)
- Right speech (*Samma vaca*)

- Right action (*Samma kammanta*)
- Right livelihood (*Samma ajiva*)
- Right effort (*Samma vayama*)
- Right mindfulness (*Samma sati)*
- Right concentration (*Samma samadhi*)

We will instead provide our very own formula—**the 100x formula**—to help you get rid of your problems and lead a happy and content life. Our formula explains that everyone aspires to be one in a hundred—in other words, to eliminate everyone else from the competition and climb to the top, which is always narrow and lonely. Why ascend a frightening and lonely peak? Be an ocean instead, where each drop is the whole, not a component of it.

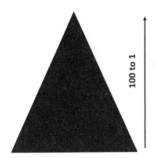

Climbing the Peak

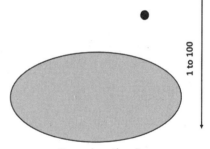

Becoming the Ocean

One, therefore, needs to just multiply oneself by 100 to succeed in life or relationships. Be the best version of yourself and improve your aptitude, skills, wealth and well-being, all at the same time.

MULTIPLY EFFORT TEN TIMES, LUCK WILL MULTIPLY 1000 TIMES. REDUCE EFFORT TEN TIMES, AND THE DOWNWARD SPIRAL WILL DIMINISH EVERYTHING YOU HAVE CREATED.

Learning 1: Many small stones make a mansion. When confused, when undecided, take one small, baby step and then the next.

Learning 2: Volatility or ups and downs are part and parcel of life and accepting this fact reduces the volatility in the mind by 99 per cent.

2

Privileged versus Not-So-Privileged

Unending Saga

Priya hastily climbed the stairs of a tall building, panting heavily. She rushed into the preoccupied hush of a large office space. The rustle of papers and the click-clack of keyboards heightened the general impression of the intensely focused workplace. But Priya was oblivious to whatever was going on around her. She made her way to the pantry, where she would prepare coffee and snacks for people who would move mountains every day from 9 a.m. to 5 p.m.

As Priya stood in the pantry, brewing coffee and arranging the snacks, she couldn't help but overhear a conversation between two employees. They were discussing the company's latest project, and Priya was amazed at how easily they were able to articulate their thoughts and ideas. She longed to be part of such discussions, to be able to express her ideas clearly and to be taken seriously.

She often spent her hours coming up with wildly different guesses about how much these people earned. 'These people work so hard, and the way they jabber non-stop in such fluent English, I'm sure they're making good money,' she would muse. She knew that one of her most useful traits was the ability to work hard, but what if she could also talk like them?

'Wouldn't that be life-changing?' she asked herself.

Three Obsolescence-Free Skills

The advantages Priya saw English bestowing upon workers compelled her to learn and master the language—she was intelligent enough to figure out this was the only way to earn more money. Priya's actions echo what Napoleon Hill mentions in his famous book, *Think and Grow Rich*, 'Whatever your mind can conceive and believe, it can achieve'.

Dominion of Discipline

Discipline is the key here. Life management and money management have the same node at the inflection point, and that's discipline. Discipline does not mean having a good work day every day or having the same intensity every day; discipline simply means showing up every day, whether it is a good day or a tough day.

Whether it's life, relationships, investing or making money, emotional intelligence is more important than intellectual intelligence.

> DISCIPLINE IS THE STRONGEST SHIELD AGAINST ANY UNSEEN EVENTUALITY AND THE STEALTHIEST WEAPON AGAINST ANY ADVERSARY.

Hope, Possibilities, Setbacks

Priya was determined to master the English language, and she did it successfully. However, when the thought of learning English had first struck her, excitement filled Priya's innocent heart and she felt an insistent drive to change her destiny. With a thumping heart full of resolution and adrenalin, she walked over to her boss, who had been rambling about a failed deal for nearly an hour. Priya had been patiently waiting for him to hang up the phone. She approached him with utmost humility when the call ended and told him about her desire to learn the language. She had always admired his ability to articulate and present his case persuasively and effectively. Hesitantly, she said, 'I want to talk like you, sir. I want to learn English.'

'English?' he snickered and continued, 'Why would you want to learn English? You're doing a good job here. And we're paying you enough. You don't need to waste your time learning English. Continue to focus on your work.' Priya had been promised a raise of Rs 5,000 within the first month of her employment. It was her fifth month on the job, and she was still being paid the same amount of money.

He continued, 'You know, Priya,' and here he took a long pause, trying to look like he was considering his words, 'English is not your language. You'll never be able to speak it proficiently, like an expert. You have come from a vernacular medium school and hence, however hard you try, you will fail. It's better for you to focus on doing what you are doing and getting paid for your petty job. Don't bother yourself with these imaginary goals, it's a waste of time.'

Disheartened and disappointed by the response, Priya left quietly. As she walked away, her boss's mocking tone echoed in her ears, filling her with frustration and anger. She felt embarrassed and ashamed for even mentioning the thought of learning English.

In a fit of self-pity, she wondered how her life would have been if she had the privilege of getting better schooling, a better education, slightly better resources.

Is education a privilege, then?

Education is a fundamental right—Article 21A of the Constitution of India makes provision for free and compulsory education for all children between six and fourteen years of age. The fundamental nature of the right entails the right to be taught, to learn and to hone one's skills and capabilities. However, it is an undeniable fact that access to quality education is not universal because of the 'privilege gap' in the world.

Priya was taken aback by her boss's response. She had always looked up to him as a role model, and his belittling remark had left her feeling dejected and downcast. She had grown up in a small village where education was considered a luxury, and those who could afford it were looked up to with awe and admiration. She had always dreamt of being able to speak fluent English, but she had never had the opportunity to learn it.

> BAD DAYS ARE A GIVEN, AS ARE GOOD DAYS. THE RESILENT PERSON TAKES MINUTES TO RECUPERATE WHERE THE AVERAGE HUMAN TAKES WEEKS.

Her boss's condescending attitude only served to reinforce the idea that education was something that only the privileged could acquire. It was a bitter pill to swallow, but Priya refused to let it dampen her spirits. She knew that if she wanted to succeed in life, she would have to work twice as hard as those who had had the benefit of a good education or connections, both made possible by wealth. She had to narrow and eventually close this gap between herself and the privileged.

What is a 'privilege gap'?

The privilege gap stems from a lack of money and other resources. Students born into upper-class or upper-middle-class families with connections have early exposure to the language of success, allowing them to develop superior communication skills and confident personalities. Such children learn the sophisticated articulation of English right from birth from hearing the adults in their home, who themselves have had the privilege of an expensive private school education. Of course, there are always outliers who force this gap closed, the self-made ones who, through endless toil or charm or a talent for finding loopholes or simply greasing the right palm at the right time, break through the barrier and muscle their way into the ranks of the privileged. But for most, the gap is insurmountable.

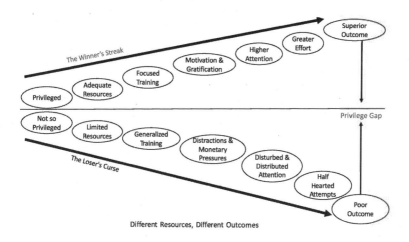

Different Resources, Different Outcomes

The external environment

One of the significant factors that contribute to this gap is the environment in which children are brought up. As mentioned earlier, children born into affluent families have access to better facilities and resources that aid in their cognitive, emotional and social development. They are also exposed to a wider range of experiences, such as travel, cultural events and activities that enhance their communication skills and confidence.

Furthermore, the children of wealthy families tend to interact with people who are also privileged, including entrepreneurs, politicians, lawyers and industrialists. These people are more willing to share their knowledge during conversations, which then gives these children a significant advantage in their education and future careers. Additionally, privileged children may have more opportunities to network with successful individuals who can help them in their professional lives.

An example of this would be students of elite schools such as the Doon School or Mayo College. These schools are known for educating the children of affluent families, including the kids of politicians, business people and other influential individuals. One of the most useful things about the schooling at such institutions is that they encourage kids to make friends and build networks with each other. Connections made with other affluent and influential individuals in childhood prove particularly useful in these students' careers later in life. The relationships formed in these schools often result in mutual favours and the signing of mutually beneficial contracts when these children grow up.

While it's true that not everyone has the same level of access to privilege and opportunities, some individuals work hard to attain desirable goals, lifestyles and outcomes for themselves. This path is arduous and requires constant self-motivation especially when there is no external assistance.

> CONNECTIONS CAN BE A PRIVILEGE, BUT OBSERVATION, APPLICATION OF KNOWLEDGE AND GAINING WISDOM ARE A CHOICE.

Few people take this difficult path to achieve one's dream life. Ultimately, the choice lies with the individual.

The Common Denominator and the Higher Factor

The ultimate aim of the human being, according to various saints, sages and psychologists, is self-actualization and to end the cycle of birth, life and death.

How can one think of self-actualization when one is worried only about survival and fulfiling one's basic needs on a daily basis, when the fundamental need of the human is not met?

Money, financial independence and substantial wealth give one the choice of whether to remain in pursuit of creating more wealth and experiencing gratification through wealth, or moving up in the hierarchy of human needs and pursuing other goals.

Once essential needs are met, people can exercise the choice of whether to pursue

> MOTIVATION IS THE BIGGEST ENABLER. CURSING, ABUSING AND PRESSURING ANOTHER WITH UNACHIEVABLE EXPECTATIONS IS THE BIGGEST DERAILMENT.

moksha (salvation) or continue pursuing the gratification of the senses. Thus, people can be divided into two kinds: those who go with the flow of the river to finally join the ocean one day, and those who are curious to find out what lies at the end of a never-ending ocean. Being the former is pure bliss, but the latter comes with perpetual pain.

These two kinds of people emerge from different perspectives and have different priorities. Those who go with the flow are content with the status quo and find peace in living a simple life. They may value stability, security and predictability, and prioritize their comfort and well-being over taking risks or exploring the unknown.

On the other hand, those who are curious to find out what lies at the end of a never-ending ocean are often driven by a thirst for knowledge, adventure and discovery. They may prioritize personal growth, exploration and new experiences over comfort and stability.

The reasons why some people are content with becoming one with the ocean, while others seek adventure and the unknown, can be complex and multifaceted.

It can depend on a variety of factors, including personality traits, life experiences, upbringing, culture and societal expectations. Some individuals may have a natural inclination towards exploration and curiosity, which drives them to seek out new experiences and knowledge. These individuals may possess traits such as openness to experience, creativity and a sense of adventure.

In contrast, as mentioned earlier, others may value security, stability and predictability, which may lead them to prefer a more settled and routine lifestyle. These individuals may have a greater need for control and may prioritize comfort and familiarity over taking risks and exploring the unknown.

Upbringing and culture can also play significant roles in shaping one's values and priorities. For example, individuals raised in a family or culture that values tradition, conformity and adherence to established norms may be more likely to prefer a settled and predictable lifestyle.

One must reiterate the fact that until basic monetary needs are met, the focus remains stuck on earning and acquiring more money.

Priya was in exactly that situation. At that point, what Priya wanted the most was finding her identity.

What was her purpose?

What did she want to be?

Why did she leave her peaceful abode to live in this fast-paced city?

One can keep thinking about the utopian principle of existence, but when hunger and suffering dominate a person's existence, the mind becomes the master, playing the victim card rather than serving us.

> SAVINGS AND INVESTMENTS HELP IN TWO WAYS. THEY CUT EXPENDITURE ON THINGS. SECOND, SAVINGS PROVIDE A SENSE OF SECURITY AND ENABLE ONE TO EXPLORE MORE AND TAKE FUTURE RISKS. WHY SPEND ON THINGS WE DO NOT NEED TO IMPRESS PEOPLE WE DON'T LIKE?

The answer was simple: financial freedom.

What Does Financial Freedom Mean?

Most people believe that financial freedom means having enough money and resources that will allow one to pursue what one likes.

However, it's much deeper. Every person is short of a few things—time, human bandwidth and the attention that one wishes to give.

Financial freedom means that one becomes the master of one's own focus, with attention not being devoted only to earning money, managing money or growing money—

money itself works for the person like a servant and ensures that their goals are met. A simple way to achieve financial freedom is:

Passive income > active income > yearly expenses

> ON THIS PLANET, ONLY TWO THINGS ARE LIMITED: CAPITAL AND HUMAN BANDWIDTH. IF CAPITAL CAN MULTIPLY AND RELEASE YOUR PRECIOUS BANDWIDTH, IMAGINE THE POSSIBILITIES YOU CAN HAVE.

Priya grew up in a small village, where her mother worked as domestic help to make ends meet. Her father passed away when she was young, making her mother the sole breadwinner of the family. Despite her mother's tireless efforts, the family struggled to make ends meet, and Priya had to grow up quickly to help her mother with household chores and take care of her younger siblings.

As Priya grew older, she started to question her life and her purpose. She saw how her mother worked hard every day, yet they barely had enough for their basic needs. She saw how her younger siblings struggled to get a good education and how their dreams were often curtailed due to lack of resources. She knew that there had to be more to life than this.

Priya's curiosity and desire for something more led her to leave her peaceful abode and move to the fast-paced city. She knew that it would be a difficult journey, but she was willing to take the risk. She wanted to find her identity and her purpose, to make a better life for herself and her family.

> YOU ARE YOUR BEST MOTIVATIONAL SPEAKER. TRY ONCE, AND YOU WILL NEVER REGRET.

But she needed direction to find the answers to these questions, someone who could guide her towards a path that was meant for her. Unfortunately, she had nobody. She was lost and clueless. Imagine the feeling of being lost on a mountain or an island where there is no obvious trail leading to your destination. This is exactly how she felt.

While hiking or trekking for the first time in snow-clad mountains which are thousands of feet above sea level, there are certain thoughts that may cross one's mind, especially for someone who's an amateur hiker:

'Oh, what if I get lost?'

'What if I come across a snow leopard?'

'How long will it take to reach the summit?'

'Will I be able to reach the base camp before dawn?'

'If not, how will I make it to base camp during the night?'

Not only are these thoughts intimidating, they are all also sensible, justifiable reasons to worry.

The Mentor, the Coach, the Guide

Hence, it's always advised that hikers hire a local guide while trekking in hilly areas. The guide won't do the trek for you, of course, but will help make your journey safe and devoid of unnecessary hindrances that may come your way. They will mentor you about the dos and don'ts before you begin your trek. They will advise against doing anything that may harm you physically, mentally and emotionally. They will have checked that you have taken all precautions before letting you take your first step and most importantly, they will keep motivating you at every step before you make it to the summit.

Life is a journey and having a guide on this journey makes it a bit easier and smoother. Many of the celebrities you follow have probably struggled a lot in their initial days, but these people might all tell you they had this one person in their lives who helped make them what they are today.

Take, for instance, the story of **Lata Mangeshkar**.

SETBACKS SET THE TONE FOR SUCCESS. THE HIGHER THE NUMBER OF SETBACKS, THE GREATER THE PROBABILITY OF SUCCESS.

Also known as the 'nightingale of India', Lata Mangeshkar sang over 25,000 songs. The song, *'Meri awaaz hi meri pehchaan hai'* truly defines her admirable and successful journey. However, while her songs and her voice remain legendary and evergreen, there was a time when she was rejected for the same voice. It was considered too pitchy by industry standards at the time and hence, she faced many rejections during her early working years.

But there was this one music director who showed great faith in Lata's capabilities and because of whom, Lata got a break in the Hindi film industry. His name was Master Ghulam Haider, one of the legendary music directors of the Hindi film industry. In an interview, Lata ji recalled how Master Ghulam Haider fought for her and showed complete faith in her talent when everyone had rejected her. She said,

'Ghulam Haider is truly my Godfather. It was his confidence in me that he fought for me to tuck me into the Hindi Film Industry, which otherwise had rejected me.'[1]

---

[1] 'Lata Mangeshkar Admitted "Ghulam Haider Is Truly My Godfather"', *Ceylon Mirror*, 8 February 2022, available at ceylonmirror.net/english/10133.html.

Today, Lata ji is remembered for her melodious voice, but the story that we know today may have been different if her talent was never acknowledged by anyone. You can call it luck that someone like Master Haider was there to support her. It's not as if she would've been nothing if it wasn't for her godfather—of course, her talent and hard work

> GO FOR A GURU, SEEK A MENTOR, CATCH A COACH. JUST AS ONE NEEDS HELP NAVIGATING AN UNCHARTED PATH, THE MENTOR IS ALSO LOOKING FOR BRIGHT PROTÉGÉS TO CARRY ON THEIR LEGACY.

would've paved the way for her success sooner or later. But having a mentor or a godfather like Master Ghulam Haider surely saved her some trouble.

If Master Ghulam Haider hadn't trusted Lata's abilities and talent, the nightingale would have remained in anonymity.

There are many such stories. Sometimes, the mentor shows the path, sometimes they help tread that path and sometimes they prevent one from veering off course. There are a variety of ways, some subtle and some explicit, in which a mentor guides one to reach their full potential.

Sachin Tendulkar, who has a total of 34,357 runs in international cricket, a record that is unlikely to be surpassed any time soon, was taught by the late Ramakant Achrekar.

Sachin has always professed his gratitude for the guidance and coaching Achrekar gave him and said he owes his legendary career to Achrekar.

In one of his interviews with PTI (Press Trust of India), Sachin revealed how Achrekar's hard smack for missing a match completely changed his life.

> After finishing school, I used to hurry to my aunt's place for
> lunch and by that time, sir used to organise some matches

> FREQUENT CHANGES IN GOALPOSTS REFLECT FICKLE-MINDEDNESS RATHER THAN FLEXIBILITY.

for me. He used to tell the opposition teams, that I would be batting at No. 4.

On one such day, instead of playing in the match, I along with a friend, went to the Wankhede stadium to watch the Shardashram English-medium boys take on the Shardashram Marathi-medium boys in the Harris Shield final and cheer our team.

There, we spotted sir and went to greet him. He knew that I had missed the match, but still asked me how did I perform in it. I told him that, I thought that I would skip the match in order to cheer for our team. I got a late-cut (tight slap) on my face as well. The tiffin box in my hand flew and all its contents spread across.

At that time, sir told me 'You don't have to be here to cheer for others. Play in such a way that others cheer for you.' Since that day, I began practising very hard and put in a lot of hours. If not for that day, I might have been cheering others from the stands.[2]

> EXPERTISE IS BUILT BY REPETITION. REPETITION CREATES MUSCLE MEMORY. MUSCLE MEMORY BRINGS EASE, CONFIDENCE AND CONTROL.

A mentor not only guides one towards the right path, but also makes sure that one doesn't deviate from that path. Sometimes, even when one is aware of the steps to be taken to achieve their goals, they may take things for granted and procrastinate. This is unproductive—there will be

---

[2] 'How a Ramakant Achrekar slap shaped Sachin Tendulkar's career', *Hindustan Times*, 3 January 2019, available at https://www.hindustantimes.com/cricket/how-a-ramakant-achrekar-slap-shaped-sachin-tendulkar-s-career/story-klK IkPOF9HewEWuWsuO4QI.html.

no results till one actively pursues one's goals. Consistency is the key and consistency comes with discipline. And a true mentor makes sure that discipline is upheld.

Warren Buffet–Benjamin Graham

Warren Buffet is one of the most renowned protégés of the father of value investing, Benjamin Graham. One of the most important lessons that Buffet learnt from Graham is 'doing something foolish'. Generally, foolish is a word that is used with a negative connotation, but Graham explained to Buffet that humility and willingness to forego self-importance are important to learning and succeeding. Markets are bigger than every participant and ego cannot get in the way when one experiences failure.

Ego in the market, ego in life and ego in relationships is the biggest derailer, creating a roadblock to one's success.

What happens to others who don't get mentors?

Don't they aspire to work hard and be recognized for their talent?

Few people coming from modest backgrounds make it big and have mentors to coach, guide and hone their talent; what about the others?

Not everyone is lucky or privileged enough to have a mentor in their lives. Some people just have it the hard way and that's what life is. Like these people, Priya had no godfather, no clear purpose and no innate talent. This made her anxious. For her, it felt as if time was passing in the blink of an eye and she was stuck in this office, serving coffee to white-collared employees.

While she was pondering her current situation, a man in his late thirties knocked on the coffee counter slab. Startled by the sound, Priya murmured, 'What would you like to . . .?' Before she could complete her question, the man interrupted her and said, 'I would like to offer you a job at my office, which is on the third floor of this building.' She couldn't fathom what just happened and was so confused that she couldn't utter a word for the next few seconds. 'Who is this person and why is he offering me a job out of the blue?' she asked herself.

'I heard you were in dire need of money and were looking for a part-time job, and we could use someone like you for this role, so let me know your decision whenever you're ready,' he said. Again, she just didn't understand what was going on and how to respond to any of that. The man left. Priya was left confused and felt a tinge of hope and excitement inside her.

She went back home that day and was awake till 3 a.m. She kept asking herself, 'Should I take this job? It's an opportunity that may never come again. I'll be able to save money and maybe this job could help me find my purpose.' These thoughts kept circling inside her mind and she had no idea how to deal with them. She had nobody to take a suggestion from; all she could do was listen to her heart and go ahead with her decision.

So the next day, the elevator stopped at the third floor, and right in front of her was another office that looked just like the one where she worked, but with fewer people. She sat down on a sofa placed in the waiting area. As soon as she saw the man who had offered her the job, she got up with a smile and hope in her eyes and told him that she would like to work part-time. The man greeted her warmly and told her that she would have to go through on-the-job training since she had no experience with their work. Priya was absolutely euphoric. It seemed as if things were finally falling into place.

She always desired to have a skill that could help her make enough money. But the only problem was that she could never understand what skill she wanted to have and how to acquire it. And here, they were going to train her and pay her for learning things that would help her make a career for herself! She felt lucky and a bit nervous at the same time. She was nervous because of the apprehension that she might not perform well and they might throw her out. Priya was underconfident, but she was also determined to give her best.

Leaning 1: Life will throw stones (sometimes directly, sometimes indirectly). Let them not go to waste. Keep collecting them, they will one day form the platform for your launchpad.

Learning 2: The best thing in life is to find a genuinely good friend. The next best thing is to find a good coach and a mentor. If both are not happening, don't struggle, let the environment and the universe be your mentor and everything else fall into place.

3

Why Move from 1 to 100 and Not from 100 to 1?

The Dilemma of Success

Have your ever wondered, if everyone was a winner, who would the loser be?
Would winning have any meaning then?

Is life entirely black and white, or is it grey?

It's a matter of perspective. For example, some may believe in the idea that everyone can be successful, while others may find it too good to be true. **Pause and think about it. How do you feel about success?**

The idea of everyone being a winner raises questions about the meaning and significance of winning itself. If everyone's a winner, then victory loses its value and meaning. The thought that you can either be a winner or a loser may lead some people to doubt themselves. These people think they are not good enough to achieve success and, therefore, feel demotivated to strive for excellence.

However, as mentioned earlier, life is not entirely black and white; it is full of grey areas. There is no one-size-fits-all approach to success. What may work for one person may not work for another.

Success is a journey, and it is essential to find out what it means to you personally. Hence, **define and achieve *your* version of success,** so that you can lead a fulfiling and meaningful life.

Most of us desire to come out on top, to be part of the top **1 per cent.**

What is it to be in the top 1 per cent?

Being wealthier and happier, having more friends and great relationships, creating a legacy to leave behind, controlling the resources of this planet or being recognized by other people for one's good work.

What is that 1 per cent?

Usually, people think that getting to the top means finding their way or pushing other people behind—*leaving the 99 per cent behind and rising above them.* **The conundrum is that to be called that 1 per cent, one still needs the other 99. Hence, one will always need that 99 per cent.**

Why think in terms of a mountain, which keeps growing narrower as one rises to the top—fewer relationships, fewer friends, less happiness, less freedom and less time?

Can one think in terms of becoming the ocean instead?

Doesn't a drop have an ocean inside it and doesn't an ocean have several drops in it?

When one thinks of leading, it means taking everyone along, ensuring that the collective well-being improves by the collective action of many, which may be initiated by one, but is executed by and beneficial to many.

Segregated Approach versus Conjoint Approach (*Ekatmik*)

1 to 100 or 100 to 1?

What is the most fundamental law of nature? **To multiply.** Nature supports that which yields growth, proliferation and multiplication.

The good multiplies, and so does the bad. When the bad multiplies, it harms everyone else, eventually destroying or reducing creation itself and hence, it can't persist.

A student learns, practises, improvises, experiences and then instructs in order to multiply what they have learnt as well as to increase others' knowledge. An individual who starts as a student and eventually emerges a teacher is the very image of proliferation.

A seed, when sown, multiplies through sunlight and water into several leaves, branches and a thick trunk. It then bears fruits and the fruits have several seeds. Each seed then multiplies into several trees and many more fruits, and thus a forest is created.

Peaks are temporary, oceans are permanent. Peaks get eroded and new peaks are formed through the movement and compression of the earth's tectonic plates. However, the oceans just expand.

Simply put, this is what it means when it is said that one should move from 1 to 100.

Multiply the effect, multiply the impact and multiply yourself by creating several others who are prosperous, thriving and well-heeled like you.

Some argue that if everyone is to be equal, why are focus, dedication, hard work, perseverance and effort required?

WHY THINK OF BEING A PYRAMID ON WHICH, WHEN ONE ELEMENT— EITHER FAME, MONEY OR RELATIONSHIP—APPEARS, THE REST VANISHES? BE AN OCEAN WHERE EVERYTHING MULTIPLIES.

Diversity is the law of nature. Despite several seeds coming from the same fruit, being sown in the same soil and being provided with the same amount of water, different seeds bear different qualities of fruit and grow into trees of different sizes.

Happiness and satisfaction come when one multiplies. That's why everyone looks at growing their business and successive generations are expected to take it further.

The stock market, or listed equities, constitutes one such platform on which many can win together. If they control their greed, their fear and their biases, together, they can win. They can even stop the wrongdoing of a large institution or the ill-advised actions of a corporate honcho who may be thinking of short-term goals driven by their own short-term motives, sometimes short-changing the minority shareholders.

In the markets, in life, in investing and in relationships, most people spend their time and energy on defeating others to get ahead. Everyone's endeavour is to pull others down and make themselves look good. This kind of behaviour is, in fact, self-defeating. We will explain why pulling down others is a sign of self-sabotage.

> JEALOUSY OCCURS BECAUSE OTHERS EXIST. JEALOUSY ARISES BECAUSE ONE WISHES TO SHOW OFF TO OTHERS. WHY COMPETE WITH OTHERS, SHOW OFF TO OTHERS? COMPETING WITH SELF BRINGS IMPROVEMENT AND HAPPINESS.

Why?

Jealousy is one of the prime reasons for many, or most, conflicts. Jealousy arises from the emotion of fear. Any act that is done in fear is never rewarding. Fear is a good emotion when there is an immediate question of survival, but eventually, as adaptability, familiarity and expertise develop, that emotion of fear should be discarded in favour of a love of the act.

It's ironic that millions of people invest in equity markets without any expert advice, putting their hard-earned money directly into businesses despite having no understanding of those businesses, and yet believe they can win.

Most investors who invest with no domain knowledge are unable to even beat inflation during a decade or two decade-long investment period, adjusting for corporate action.

Thus, one should always look for a journey rather than moving from 100 to 1 among them, comparing oneself with everyone and trying to beat or outperform them all.

Can the needs of two identical twins be the same in life and in investments? The answer is no. Then why compare and sulk?

It's tragic that the same act, event or situation that gives pleasure when engaged in for its own sake, causes pain when you start to compare yourself with others.

Two Perspectives: **Individualistic or Ekatmik (Conjoint)**

There is a *shlok* from an ancient Upanishad:

ॐ

पूर्णमदःपूर्णमिदं पूर्णात् पूर्णमुदच्यते।
पूर्णस्य पूर्णमादाय पूर्णमेवावशिष्यते

That (the visible outer world) is full, this (the invisible inner world) is also full. From that fullness comes this fullness, taking away this fullness from that fullness, fullness indeed remains.

In simple words, the universe is complete and whole. Taking anything out of it will not reduce it and it will continue to remain full.

What changes or transforms is only the form!

There are two ways of looking at any situation or at any monetary aspect.

a. <u>Individualistic approach:</u> This approach suggests that when one does their best and tends to maximize one's own well-being, the overall well-being of the group improves.

But is it true?

In the process of maximizing one's own well-being, one goes to any extent possible and thus creates rifts through power play. One might win, but only at the expense of the other.

When the one who loses returns to the fray from a defeat, they tend to do more harm, and thus the cycle of destruction and annihilation continues.

It's sad but true that roughly two-thirds of IPOs, even a couple of years after listing, remain underwater or below their issue price.

Why does this happen?

The promoter of a company, at the time of its listing, tends to extrapolate earnings to arrive at and justify an aggressive issue price. However, when the realistic day-to-day performance of the company surfaces, the stock corrects itself. Furthermore, it is the merchant banker who is incentivized on higher listing and thus, the minority shareholders are the ones who bear the brunt of losses.

In the long term, the valuation of the company dips, eroding the net worth of the promoter as well as value for minority shareholders.

On the other hand, if one creates an environment where everyone's interests are aligned and one's gain does not mean another one's pain, wouldn't life, relationships and investing all be seamless?

What if the merchant banker leaves some money on the table for the minority shareholder to experience the joy of making money? What if the promoter cleans up their act a few years before the listing, as a listing entails close public scrutiny, and works towards growth that is consistent instead of rapid?

Do businesses that scale up to 100 times in about twenty years focus on greed or on consistency and enhanced efficiency?

If the business supports the ecosystem during tough economic periods, if the business rewards minority shareholders for trusting the business during untoward times, if the business is watchful and prepared for unforeseen disruptions and challenges, it is more likely to scale up and create wealth.

This is all governed by **processes, frameworks and methodologies** that the smart human resources team of the firm set up and they keep adapting to changes in the environment. **This mirrors the way nature works—nature creates and nature regulates, all through a pre-established process.**

An established process controls not only excessive greed but also wastage of resources. These resources, when used optimally, lead to consistency, and consistency, with a clean approach, leads to success and wealth creation.

b. <u>Ekatmik or Conjoint Approach</u> is one where everyone and everything is believed to be conjoint, interlinked and interdependent, and thus one uses and utilizes resources as per one's requirements and needs, rather than one's greed.

Legends always create interdependence and linkages with the environment as the change in the environment is constant, and that should not hamper the chances of combined success and well-being.

One of the greatest rulers of Bharat, who consolidated large swathes of the land under one rule, was Chandragupta Maurya.

Can his life provide some lessons for life, investing or relationships in the modern world?

Chandragupta Maurya was one of the greatest emperors, the one who laid the foundations of the Maurya dynasty and unified Bharat, from the Kabul River Valley in the west to modern-day Bengal in the east. He defeated the Greek successor of Alexander, Seleucus I Nicator, to win and control Alexander's Asian empire. He was taught and nurtured by the greatest guru in post-Vedic Indian history, Chanakya.

The great emperor had everything—resources and aides—to fulfil all his wishes, and yet he fasted unto death.

Why?

During his reign, Chandragupta undertook mega irrigation, road and mining projects and built beautiful temples and palaces so people in his kingdom could prosper. His focus was always on the welfare of his people. But destiny had something else in store for his empire. Despite all his efforts and a modern irrigation infrastructure, the kingdom faced famines over successive years. The drought became so severe that barely any food was available for the common man living in his kingdom.

Seeing the plight of his people and with no solution in sight, Chandragupta renounced the world, handing over the reins of the kingdom to his son Bindusara, and fasted unto death.

Why did Chandragupta Maurya take this step?

He believed that there was no difference between him and the common person in his kingdom. He was ekatmik, conjoint, united with all the people living in his kingdom, and thus felt their plight and went through the same fate as many in his kingdom.

Greatness or richness is not achieved by building palaces on graveyards, but by impacting lives even hundreds and thousands of years after one has left this world and returned to dust.

The Greatness of Shivaji Maharaj

Another great general was Shivaji Maharaj, whose desire to establish Hindavi Swaraj ignited the spirit of bravery, camaraderie and companionship between him and the men who shared the same dream. Just 350 years ago, he unified Bharat from the tip of the Indus River covering Attock, Peshawar and Kashmir in the North to Tiruchirappalli, Tanjavur in the South. From Cuttack to Kandla the flag of the Marathas flew high. Shivaji sowed the seeds and created an ecosystem that was taken ahead by successive generations to create one of the greatest empires in history.

How did Shivaji manage to establish such a vast empire in a short time? Are there any lessons to be learnt from the great Maratha warrior in investing?

The answer again lies in multiplying oneself from 1 to 100. Shivaji's commanders were as daring, as courageous and as dedicated as he was. To name a few, Yesaji carried a sword that was 65 kg of pure metal and once lifted, it was sure to bring enemies' heads down. Another such force that enabled the establishment of the Hindavi Swaraj was Santaji Ghorpade, who could travel from Delhi to Pune, a distance of 1170 km, in 7 hours on a horse. **Sambhaji,** popularly known as Shambhuraje, the eldest son of Shivaji, fought about 120 battles and lost none. Ramji Pangera defeated an army of over 30,000 Mughals with merely 700 men.

Shivaji realized that sharing a common dream and common perspective would enable everyone and would help them win collectively rather than lose individually.

What if all stakeholders, including promoters, CXOs, employees, distributors, suppliers, wholesalers, retailers and the board, think collectively for the well-being of the business, and in the process, the well-being of the community and the country? Wouldn't creating wealth be easier?

Businesses that can align the interest of all stakeholders are able to create 100X wealth not only for their promoters or their employees, but also for their minority shareholders.

Marthanda Varma, the Unsung Legend and the Formidable Force of South India

In the early eighteenth century, the Dutch East India Company, a formidable force in the trading world, had established its dominance along the Malabar coast. Exploiting local rulers and kingdoms, they kept a tight grip on the lucrative trade routes. Their arrogance knew no bounds; they believed no one could challenge their supremacy.

In 1741, a battle erupted on the shore in a small coastal village called Colachel. The Dutch ships unleashed a barrage of cannon fire upon the Travancore forces. Despite being outnumbered, the Travancore troops skilfully manoeuvred their smaller vessels, swiftly dodging the incoming cannonballs.

As the battle reached its climax, the Dutch ships, battered and outnumbered, retreated in defeat. These forces were led by Marthanda Varma, the ruler of Travancore, a small kingdom in Kerala.

Marthanda Varma had modernized his army and trained his soldiers in European tactics. In 1741, he led his forces in the Battle of Colachel, defeating the Dutch and ending their monopoly. It was the first time the Dutch had been defeated by an Asian power.

This also led to the collapse of the Dutch East India Company, which had control over large parts of Africa, ceding access of India and Africa to its then-rival British East India Company.

A small regional power can outpace, scuttle or tear down a giant. In the modern day, we call this disruption. But disruption is not about technology alone, as the latest technology and the resources required to buy it and adopt it quickly are available more readily to a behemoth corporation than to a small business. But some play it differently using their strength and determination and thus emerge successful. That's how a very small number of businesses—about three out of 1000—go from being small cap to large cap in a decade.

The factors common to the greatest regimes, the greatest emperors and the greatest dynasties that have existed on the planet are as follows:

1. Spirit of growth
2. Pacing progress and spreading it all across, to everyone
3. Compassion and wholesomeness
4. Consistency
5. High degree of morality and pursuing the path of dharma
6. All in or all out
7. Focused, concentrated approach
8. Constant learning
9. Continued improvement and improvization
10. Courage and fearlessness

Is it any different in investing? Perhaps not. Businesses also show similar characteristics.

But can all these traits also be exhibited by the common individual? The answer is yes.

For any great outcome, there are aspects that one needs to take into consideration.

- Character
- Thoughts
- Action

They are all interlinked and essential for a mammoth task to be accomplished.

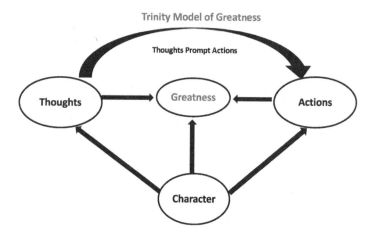

Thought gives rise to action, but action is difficult to sustain without character—in tough times, it easy to drop the action midway, or even close to the target, without strength of character. Despite having a strong character, there will be no productive action without thought and one might suffer stagnation, moving stolidly on the same path with little change. Equally, thoughts may emerge with great positivity and the best intent, but if they don't translate into the first step, or action, thoughts and character are both wasted.

> ILL-INTENDED ACTIONS WILL LEAD TO BAD OUTCOMES— SOMETIMES SOONER, SOMETIMES LATER.

How are great thoughts, actions and character built? Before exploring further, let's figure out what thoughts are.

Thoughts are bouts of energy that strike the brain and dissipate when faced with the external environment and resistance.

Waves of water rush to the shore each moment and recede in unending rhythm. Some people surf these waves, others use them for propulsion and for some, they are just a phenomenon to gaze upon. It's unfortunate that nearly three-fourths of thoughts that emerge in the human brain are residues of the past—in other words, they are rooted in experiences we have had and are resurfacing as worries.

New ideas and imaginings constitute only one-fourth of our thoughts and if they are not acted upon, they remain in the subconscious mind passively making one's belief systems, restricting one's ability to break one's barriers. Those who are able to act upon new ideas and thoughts end up changing their destiny.

The sequence of destiny is simple.

Thoughts, these bouts of energy, form one's words.

These words translate into actions.

These actions, repeated again and again, form habits.

These habits, pursued constantly, form character.

Character finally determines the destiny of the human.

What determines our thoughts?

The environment.

What's meant by environment?

Environment simply means the people whom one is around—their actions, behaviour, words, feelings and intents.

Most people confuse the environment with inanimate surroundings.

Yes, the inanimate environment plays a role, but what has the largest impact are living beings.

We thus find that those who have achieved greatness in any form or manner have surrounded themselves with great people consistently. Great people inspire you to become a better of version of yourself. They encourage you

to relentlessly pursue your goals and advise you to make the right changes at the right time to achieve success.

If, therefore, one is in the company of great people, they can quickly complete the cycle of understanding, execution, course correction, pivoting and moving forward and achieve phenomenal success.

After what Priya has gone through, she needed to pause and rethink, reassess and regain the courage to start over.

POR strategy

Whenever one is confused, overwhelmed or muddled, adopt the POR strategy.

- ✓ **P—Pause:** Take a break or simply stop. Figure out where you started, where you have reached and from which direction. The best way to assess the situation is by writing it down.

Writing gives clarity and specificity and brings focus back.

- ✓ **O—Open:** Open the mind and segregate your thoughts.

    Stage 1: Segregate what is controllable and what is uncontrollable. Again, writing things down can be helpful. Then focus—control **what is controllable, let what is uncontrollable go.**

PAUSES IN LIFE PERMIT ONE TO APPRECIATE THE POWER OF ACTION AND THE POWER OF CONSOLIDATION IN BOTH STRATEGY AND EFFORT.

Let go of things that can't be acted upon or where no action can be taken. Talk to yourself; inform your brain that nothing can be done about certain things and thereafter ignore them.

<u>**Tasks, when reduced, prompt one to take quick action**</u> as opposed to when the mind is cluttered with ideas and thoughts that cannot be executed or are beyond one's reach at the moment.

Stage 2: 99/1 principle—paying for peace
Only 1 per cent of things cause the greatest pain and interestingly, that 1 per cent is not even significant in the larger scheme of things.

But those 1 per cent irritants have the potential to undo 99 per cent of essential growth or positive outcomes that have been earned through hard work.

Learn to ignore the 1 per cent of nuisance factors, even if it means lowering one's ego or letting things go with a financial loss. This is a leakage, the price one should pay to buy peace, so that the remaining 99 per cent of the outcome remains enjoyable.

Stage 3: Delegate or Die
Trust is the most treasured value in human life. It can be built simply through repeated and consistent presence, without even articulating a word.

Trust others with tasks and delegate things that they can do well, even if you have proficiency in that task.

- <u>**Rejuvenate:**</u> **Delegate tasks and all of a sudden, a new stream of energy will flow in.**

Perform those tasks first that are your core competency and try to maintain this balance as you continue.

Consistency, with course correction through monitoring, leads to greatness, and that's the model for realizing 100X your own potential and that of the stock markets.

There are other examples in history where, instead of crushing others, a few collectively enriched the entire region, the entire community and the society.

Roman Journey of 1 to 100 or 100 to 1

One day, a young man was walking through the streets of Rome when he stumbled upon a group of merchants selling exotic spices and fabrics. Intrigued, he struck up a conversation with them and learnt about the vast trade networks that existed beyond the borders of Rome.

Inspired by this new-found knowledge, he decided to take a risk and invest all of his savings in a trading venture. He spent several years travelling to faraway lands, trading with merchants and learning about the intricacies of international trade.

Despite facing numerous challenges along the way, including piracy, political unrest and natural disasters, he persevered and eventually became one of the wealthiest traders in entire Rome.

But he was not content with just being a successful trader. He had ambitions of greatness, and he knew that the only way to achieve his social goals was through political power. So he turned his attention to the world of politics, using his wealth and connections to gain a foothold in the Roman Senate.

Over the years, he rose through the ranks of the government, becoming one of the most powerful figures in the empire. And yet, the young man was not satisfied.

He dreamt of leaving behind a lasting legacy that would be remembered for centuries to come. So he set his sights on the ultimate prize: the title of emperor.

So, the young man made an audacious move to seize power. In 49 BCE, he led his army across the Rubicon River, declaring war on the Roman Republic itself. This move was a clear violation of the laws and traditions of Rome.

His gamble paid off. His army was fiercely loyal to him, and his bold move across the Rubicon sent shockwaves through the Roman government. *He quickly gained support from the people of Rome, who were tired of corruption and a dysfunctional republic, and he began to build a new government based on his own vision of leadership and governance.*

In the end, the young man emerged victorious, becoming the first Roman emperor, Julius Caesar. And yet, for all his strength and determination, Caesar was not immune to the fears and emotions that plagued him throughout his journey.

In ancient Rome, the political arena was marked by intense competition, where individuals fought for power and influence. Julius Caesar was one of the most successful leaders of his time, but his success did not come without competition and challenges.

As Caesar rose to power, he encountered rivals and enemies who sought to cut him down and take what he had. He had been warned by several people that there was a plot to assassinate him, but he was still determined to attend a meeting of the Roman Senate.

Sometimes, precautions aren't enough.

To ensure his safety, Caesar took several precautions. First, he ordered his personal bodyguards to accompany him to the Senate meeting. These bodyguards were his loyal soldiers who had sworn to protect him at all costs.

He also took the unusual step of wearing a specially designed breastplate under his clothes. This breastplate was made of metal and was designed to be lightweight and discreet so that it would not be noticed by anyone who saw Caesar.

Despite these precautions, the assassination happened—Caesar was stabbed to death by a group of senators led by Marcus Brutus and Gaius Cassius.

Caesar's fear of losing power and his concern for personal security demonstrates how the euphoria of success and the fear of failure are closely intertwined. His success had made him a powerful figure, but it also made him a target for those who were threatened by his influence. His extreme measures to protect himself from harm, such as wearing a hidden breastplate, show how the fear of failure can motivate individuals to take extreme measures to maintain their success and influence.

Brutus was a respected senator and a close friend of Julius Caesar, the ambitious and powerful leader of Rome. However, Brutus began to have concerns about Caesar's growing power and feared that he may become a tyrant, endangering the Roman republic.

Brutus saw Caesar as an obstacle to his goals and values, and he believed that it was necessary to remove him to protect the people of Rome. He conspired with other senators, including Cassius, to assassinate Caesar.

Sometimes, people may cut others down to get ahead in life because they believe it's an effective strategy for achieving their goals. They may see others as obstacles to their success, and view cutting them down as a means to remove those obstacles.

Additionally, they may believe that the end justifies the means and that achieving their goals is more important than

the harm caused to others. This belief could be reinforced by societal messages that prioritize individual success and winning at all costs.

But success never comes without a cost. Brutus believed that his actions were justified and that he had saved the republic from a potential dictator. However, Brutus's decision to assassinate Caesar ultimately led to negative consequences. The assassination sparked outrage and chaos in Rome, and the power vacuum created by Caesar's death led to a civil war.

As the civil war raged on, Brutus found himself on the losing side. Despite his best efforts to rally support and continue fighting for his ideals, he was eventually captured by forces loyal to Mark Antony and Octavian, Caesar's adopted heir.

Brutus stood before his captors, a broken man, realizing the tragic irony of his situation. **In his pursuit of what he believed to be right, he had become the very thing he had sought to eliminate—a symbol of betrayal and discord. The people who had once hailed him as a defender of the republic now saw him as a traitor.**

The end came swiftly for Brutus. He was brought to trial for his role in the assassination. The people, still grieving the loss of their beloved leader, demanded justice. Brutus was found guilty and condemned to a fate befitting his actions—death by suicide.

As he took his own life, Brutus pondered the choices he had made and the path he had taken. He realized that in his pursuit of cutting others down to serve his own ends, he had ultimately cut himself off from the very virtues he held dear—integrity, honour and the well-being of Rome.

The sad ending of Brutus serves as a cautionary tale and raises an important question: should one aspire to be like Brutus, who, driven by misguided ideals, cut others down and faced a tragic end?

Or should one strive to be like Julius Caesar who, despite his flaws and the challenges he faced, worked diligently to bring out the best version of himself and leave a lasting legacy while working for himself and for others too?

The answer lies in embracing a more thoughtful and logical approach. True success and greatness come not from tearing others down, but from fostering collaboration, understanding and empathy. It's important to remember that personal success shouldn't come at the expense of others and that by choosing a more compassionate path, we can leave behind a positive legacy that will be remembered and respected.

ENABLING OTHERS CREATES A HIGHER CHANCE OF ONE'S OWN SUCCESS.

This begs the question of whether arriving at the top by crushing others is better than multiplying one's success through others who benefit, and enable others, creating a chain reaction.

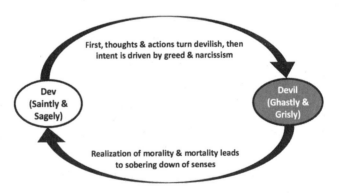

Turning from Dev to Devil or Devil to Dev

Reawakening of Priya

Priya was first awakened when she decided to leave her small hamlet and move to the big city to build a better life for her family. Now, this was her reawakening.

The universe has a funny way of enabling us. It keeps presenting us with innumerable opportunities to succeed until we have given up on ourselves.

Circling back to Priya and her ordeal

That day, when she resigned from her second job within forty-five days because her boss touched her inappropriately and made lewd remarks about her, Priya returned home with tears in her eyes and a sense of hopelessness. The thought of not having any source of income was unbearable. She longed to escape. The feeling was overpowering.

As she lay on her bed, memories of her mother flooded her mind. She would always tell Priya, 'You can go far enough by seeking advice and help from others, but you won't be able to go any further if you don't follow your own instincts.'

Those words struck a chord within her. Why had she allowed herself to be so naive, allowing others to take advantage of her vulnerability? Why would anyone approach her and give her a job just like that? This should have raised a doubt in her mind, but her naivety had clouded her wisdom.

She should have listened to her instincts the very first time she felt uncomfortable. But what was done was done. Determined, she got up, opened her window and let the cool breeze wash over her. It felt rejuvenating. With that, she wiped her tears and prepared to break free from the suffocating grip of her circumstances.

The next morning was going to be challenging for Priya. She had been searching for jobs for quite a while now, but luck seemed to elude her. Today's effort was crucial, as she only had Rs 2500 in her bank account. If she didn't secure a job today, she would have to return to her village, and her dreams of achieving greatness would be shattered.

She arrived at a small cafe for an interview for the position of a waitress. The aroma of freshly brewed coffee filled the air as she entered. Priya greeted the manager with a warm smile, trying her best to exude confidence. The interview process was rigorous, with questions about her previous experience and customer-service skills. Priya answered with honesty and enthusiasm, showing her determination to excel in her role.

Impressed by her sincerity and eagerness to learn, the manager offered Priya the job. Her heart swelled with gratitude and relief. This was the lifeline she desperately needed. She gratefully accepted the offer, feeling a renewed sense of hope.

After returning home that day, she slept for three hours straight. The sleep felt heavenly. She had been anxious about finding a job for two weeks, and finally, she had succeeded. As she woke up and washed her face, she looked into the mirror and reminded herself that she couldn't be a waitress forever. She needed to work on herself and strive for a better paying job. And for that, she needed to learn English and basic computer skills.

She possessed a second-hand laptop that had been gifted to her by a lady at her first job. As she opened the laptop that day, memories of her conversation with Mrs Kamala resurfaced. Mrs Kamala Seth, a senior employee at her previous workplace, had always been very friendly towards Priya, partly due to the uncanny resemblance between Priya and her late daughter. Talking to Priya made Mrs Seth feel as if she was conversing with her own daughter.

Priya remembered the episode with great clarity.

'How are you, beta?' Mrs Seth had said. Before Priya could respond, she continued, 'I overheard your conversation with Mr Gautam yesterday.'

Priya lowered her gaze in embarrassment. Kamala raised Priya's hands and placed a second-hand laptop in her arms. 'Here, this will help you learn English,' she said. Priya stared at her and then hugged her. She was so happy that tears rolled down her cheeks. After yesterday's incident, this was the last thing she was expecting. She thanked Mrs Seth profusely.

'You should leave this place as soon as possible, Priya. I see in your eyes the determination, relentless grit and passion to do something big. This laptop will help you explore everything you want to know about. It is your true mentor. Make the best use of it, my child. Oh, and here are some books that you can refer to once you have a basic grasp of English,' said Mrs Seth.

Priya came back to the present, brimming with hope. She knew exactly what she had to do now: work hard, very hard. She opened the laptop excitedly. She had trouble understanding how to use it properly at first, but eventually, she managed to figure it out. She had observed the people in her office using the laptop, and her keen observation skills allowed her to learn how to use it in just a few days. As Priya's fingers danced across the keyboard, she marvelled at the power it held. It was her gateway to knowledge, her portal to a world of possibilities.

Finally, she used an Excel sheet to create a timed plan for how she would learn English. The Excel sheet looked something like this: wake up at 4 a.m. to watch videos and practice until 7 a.m. Then, from 10 a.m. to 8:30 p.m., work. From 9 p.m. to 12 a.m., read and practise English. This plan seemed perfect.

Priya diligently followed this routine over the course of six months. She was determined to succeed in learning English. She decided to make the best use of her laptop to learn English and secure a better paying job. The next six months were a gruelling test of endurance. With no access to formal language courses or tutors, Priya had to rely on her own resourcefulness. She scoured the internet for free language learning resources and discovered a few helpful websites and YouTube channels that provided basic English lessons.

Every evening, after work, she would spend hours hunched over her second-hand laptop, absorbing as much knowledge as she could. Even at the cafe, she would engage in conversations with customers, using every opportunity to practise and improve her English skills. The customers would often mock her broken English, but she remained undeterred.

During her work shifts, whenever she found a spare moment, Priya would seize the opportunity to read books and newspapers lying around in the cafe. She devoured every word, absorbing the language and practising her reading skills. Sometimes she would come across unfamiliar words or phrases, but she never let them discourage her. Instead, she would jot them down and look them up later, eager to add them to her growing vocabulary.

Some days were especially tough as she had to work late-night shifts, leaving little time for studying. However, she refused to let these obstacles dissuade her. On days when she found little time to continue her learning, Priya pushed herself to study late at night and even early in the morning. Determined to make the most of every available moment, she would wake up before sunrise and dedicate those quiet hours to her studies. As the world slept, she delved into her English lessons, determined to expand her vocabulary and achieve fluency.

WHEN NOTHING IS WORKING, TRY EVEN HARDER AND HELP WILL COME FROM UNKNOWN QUARTERS.

The English learning journey was not without its difficulties. There were times when exhaustion threatened to overwhelm Priya, as the long hours and demanding work took their toll. But she refused to give in to weariness. She knew that every sacrifice she made, every moment of fatigue she endured, was bringing her closer to her goal.

The toughest part of Priya's learning journey was the lack of feedback and guidance. She had no one to correct her pronunciation or grammatical mistakes. But she didn't let this impede her progress. Determined to practise speaking English, she started watching English movies and TV shows with subtitles. She would repeat the dialogues out loud, mimicking the actors' accents and intonations.

Through her persistence and unwavering commitment, she gradually witnessed her English skills improving day by day. She started conversing fluently with the customers in the cafe. Even her peers were impressed by how swiftly Priya had improved. They start seeing her as an inspiration and were motivated to work on themselves too.

At the end of six months, after gaining some confidence and building up her skills, Priya started applying for better paying jobs. Her first attempts were met with disappointment. Dozens of applications were sent out, only to be met with rejection after rejection. The weight of each rejection letter felt like a blow to her spirit, threatening to crush her hopes and dreams.

But Priya refused to relinquish her dream and surrender. Each setback only fuelled the fire within her, igniting a determination that grew stronger with every rejection.

And then, one day, a glimmer of hope emerged. A call centre was hiring, and Priya saw it as a chance to break free from the chains that bound her. She meticulously prepared for the interview, researching the company and practising her responses. She knew that this opportunity was her ticket to a brighter future.

WHEN A SMALL OPENING IS GIVEN, PERSIST AND PERSEVERE SO THAT WHEN THE DOOR IS OPENED, YOU ARE WELCOMED IN.

When Priya stepped into the interview room, she grew nervous at first, but summoned every ounce of courage she possessed, willing herself to shine. She spoke with sincerity and passion, showcasing her newfound communication skills and the tenacity that had carried her through the toughest of times.

She was told that the final results of the interview would be communicated over a call in two to three days. Days passed, but the phone never rang. Doubt once again crept in, threatening to overshadow her optimism. But then, the phone finally rang, piercing the silence with a glimmer of hope. She cracked the interview and got the job.

A girl who was brought up in a vernacular medium has been hired by an American Call Centre to serve its clients in Europe.

Who Says Perseverance and Persistence Don't Pay?

When all doors are shut, a window, a hope, an opportunity emerges and that's what Priya had thought when she had met the gentleman who was quite delighted with her service and attitude during her days as a cook.

He recommended her to his office admin and finally, Priya was in a corporate office, washing utensils—mugs, lunch and breakfast plates—serving tea and coffee and photocopying papers.

Senior management may be more compassionate sometimes but she reported to the head of admin staff who was no different from her previous seniors. This one was even more prejudiced and egomaniacal as he had recently moved into a small cabin. Like all other places she had worked at, she was mocked, laughed and defrocked for her ability to ever have swift and smooth conversations in English.

After physical advancements from her boss, Priya had left her job. She had looked for multiple jobs, but with limited knowledge of English and no recommendations from past organizations, she found little success in her search.

She found work as a waitress at a cafe and devoted herself to learning English. But life continued to be rough and hostile for her. She refused to go along with the norms set by the restaurant manager who constantly sought favours and cut the salary with non-stop expletives.

Finally, after a relentless rollercoaster ride of eight months, Priya mustered up the courage to resign from her current job to start her new journey at the call centre.

The day she had resigned from the office job replayed in her mind. She had walked into her old workplace, a small office where she had worked as a lowly office girl, performing menial tasks for a boss who had often mocked her dreams of learning English. As she approached her boss's office, her heart pounded with a mix of anxiety and determination.

With newfound confidence, Priya knocked on the boss's door, and he looked up from his desk, surprised to see her. She held her head high and kept her voice steady as she said, 'Sir, I'd like to speak to you for a moment.'

The boss, accustomed to her subservience, glanced at her dismissively. 'What do you want, Priya? I'm busy,' he snapped.

Summoning all her courage, Priya spoke with unwavering conviction, 'I've come to hand in my formal resignation. I left

> WHEN THEY LAUGH AT YOU, REMEMBER, YOU ARE STRIVING HARD TO STAND AGAINST THE CROWD AND YOU ARE ABOUT TO WIN.

that day without notifying you, but I wanted to put the record straight and thus wanted to hand in my resignation formally.'

The boss's eyes widened, disbelief etched on his face. He struggled to comprehend the situation, momentarily unable to find words.

As the boss regained his composure, he tried to belittle her once again.

'Resignation? I don't need your resignation. Anyway, you were fired from your job! Who do you think you are? You're nothing but a girl from the slums.'

Priya stood her ground, her voice clear and strong. 'I may have come from humble beginnings, but I am not defined by them. I have worked hard to improve myself, and I have acquired valuable skills. I deserve respect, I deserve better opportunities and I deserve not to be with creeps and clowns like yourself. I need an acknowledgement that I have submitted my formal resignation to you.'

Her words hung in the air, leaving the boss speechless. His mockery turned to astonishment as he finally saw the determination and strength within Priya. In that powerful moment, Priya's resilience and self-belief shone brightly. The boss, taken aback by her unexpected transformation, had no choice but to accept her resignation, defeated by the strength she exuded.

Leaving the office that day, Priya felt an immense sense of liberation. She had reclaimed her dignity, defied the limitations imposed on her and taken a bold step towards a brighter future. Her journey was far from over, but in that pivotal moment, she realized the true power of perseverance, self-improvement and the unwavering belief in one's own potential.

With her head held high, Priya walked out of the office, leaving behind a stunned boss and an environment that had stifled her aspirations for far too long. The road ahead would still be challenging, but armed with her newfound confidence, she knew she could overcome any obstacle that came her way.

On the morning of Priya's first day at the call centre, her heart fluttered with a mix of excitement and nervousness. This job paid her three times what she was earning at her office job, and four times what she was getting in hand from the restaurant as the manager used to take away some money by bullying Priya. She was determined to give it her best. Her stint at the cafe had been temporary, meant for sustenance while she worked on her English.

The money was good, but this was also uncharted territory for her. However, as she stepped through the doors, Mr Rakesh Sharma, her manager, welcomed her with a warm smile and reassuring words that offered a glimmer of comfort.

The call centre was a hive of activity, with agents busily attending to customers' needs. The workplace felt foreign and daunting. Although she had worked on her communication skills, there was still a lot that she didn't know. But she was lucky this time that her manager and other colleagues, with patience and understanding, guided Priya through the intricacies of her new role. They introduced her to the systems, explained the protocols and instilled confidence in her.

As the day progressed, Priya encountered her fair share of difficulties. The pressure of calls was relentless and the pace was unforgiving. Despite her best efforts, there were moments when she stumbled. Her lack of experience was apparent.

> IN A WORLD FULL OF
> ANGST, ANXIETY AND
> HATRED, LIKEABILITY
> IS RARE AND MORE
> VALUABLE THAN IQ.
> PURSUE IT DILIGENTLY.

One day, a call came in that shook Priya to the core. The voice on the other end was filled with impatience; the customer vented his dissatisfaction about a delayed delivery of an important package. Priya listened attentively, empathizing with his frustration. She reassured him that she understood the urgency of the matter and would do everything in her power to resolve it promptly. However, as she delved into the system to gather information, she encountered unexpected roadblocks.

The more Priya tried to assist him, the more the situation seemed to spiral out of control. The system lagged, causing delays in retrieving vital details. Frustration boiled over, and the customer's anger erupted like a volcano. He lashed out at Priya, his words sharp and cutting. He accused Priya of incompetence and questioned her ability to handle even the simplest of tasks. Each verbal blow struck Priya's confidence, leaving her shaken and vulnerable.

Tears welled up in Priya's eyes as the customer's anger echoed in her ears. At that moment, she asked herself whether she had made a mistake, whether she was capable of handling the pressures and demands of the call centre environment. Her manager saw her crying and consoled her like any big brother would console his younger sister.

He knew Priya's story and empathized with her. He also admired her determination, resilience and perseverance. Rakesh reminded her of the journey she had undertaken, the obstacles she had overcome and the strength she had discovered within.

She knew that he was right and believed his words of wisdom and motivation. So, with renewed determination,

Priya sought guidance from her manager and colleagues. They offered invaluable advice, sharing their own experiences and techniques for handling difficult calls. Priya absorbed their wisdom like a sponge, determined to turn her weaknesses into strengths. She practised her communication skills diligently, honing her ability to defuse tense situations and provide effective solutions.

If every dejected and disheartened person got a sympathetic ear, a kind shoulder and words of motivation and support in times of tribulation, failure would never be able to crush the human spirit.

Days turned into weeks, and with each passing moment, Priya grew stronger. The calls became less daunting, and her confidence began to resurface. She started to handle challenging interactions with grace and composure, winning over customers with her empathy and dedication. Slowly but surely, she was regaining her footing in this unfamiliar terrain.

Finally, persistence finds a path through the deep ditch of darkness and hopelessness.

Priya's ascent had just begun.

As Priya continued her journey at the call centre, she faced the many obstacles that came her way with determination and resilience. Her hard work and dedication did not go unnoticed by her manager, Mr Rakesh, who admired her tenacity. He saw her potential and knew she had what it took to succeed.

She learnt from her colleagues and absorbed their valuable advice, incorporating it into her daily interactions. She developed a knack for handling ire, empathizing with customers and providing effective solutions. With each passing day, her skills grew stronger, and her ability to handle challenging calls improved significantly.

Priya's efforts did not go unrewarded. Recognizing her exceptional performance, the company rewarded her with a well-deserved salary hike. The increase in income brought a sense of financial stability to Priya's life. She decided to make the most of this opportunity and began diligently saving a portion of her earnings.

Priya adopted a systematic approach to saving. She set a monthly budget, allocating a specific amount towards her savings goal. By tracking her expenses and being mindful of her spending habits, she managed to save a significant portion of her income each month.

Her hard work and dedication did not stop at saving money. She continued to strive for excellence in her job. Her commitment and consistent performance caught the attention of the management team. Impressed by her dedication and positive impact on customer satisfaction, Priya was soon promoted to a higher position within the call centre.

Leaning 1: Life is like an ocean and we are drops in it. The more one connects with other drops, the more effectiveness and momentum build until it all becomes an ocean.

Learning 2: We turn to the evil in us to combat something evil, usually. It is correct that to beat something, we need the powers, strength and mindset equivalent to the adversary's, but when we compromise on our virtues, morality and compassionate heart, we face the same repercussions our adversary does.

4

Solving for Savings

Progress, promotion and a salary hike meant that Priya was moving forward in life. But financially, she had progressed only so far as to achieve sustenance—she could now afford to eat all three meals and send some money to her family.

But this was not what she left her life back in the village for. As she settled into her job at the call centre, she made a few good friends and realized that her problem was not unique—almost all her peers faced the same difficulties when it came to money. She started receiving some incentives on a quarterly basis, but that still was not enough.

Expenses rise faster, income always rises slower! Why?

Why are increases in income or salary always eaten up by exponential increases in expenses? Why do yearly, and even quarterly, bonuses fall short?

'Why?' and 'What next?' are the only questions Priya constantly asks herself, but she has no concrete answers yet.

She had not thought beyond her immediate aim which, so far, had been mere survival. But now that she was saving some money, she wondered how the money could work as hard as her, if not more. For as long as she could remember, the challenge looming over her family's and her life every

> EVERY DAY, BEFORE GOING TO BED, ASK YOURSELF THREE QUESTIONS:
> - DID I LEARN SOMETHING NEW?
> - DID I HAVE A GOOD MOMENT IN THE DAY?
> - DID MY MONEY WORK AS HARD AS I DID?

day had been money, and making a decent income to make her family comfortable was her top priority. For the first time in her life, she was being able to manage her expenses well, and they were a lot lower than what she was paid at the end of every month as salary.

She had heard about many schemes that promised investors that their money would grow 300 to 400 per cent in a year, but experience and instinct always made her suspect these claims. If these schemes really were so lucrative that in two and a half to three years, the invested amount would be multiplied ten times, why would banks and other big financial institutions not put their entire money into these? More so, why would the person offering the scheme not take dozens of personal loans and put their own money into it—why get others to be part of it? She had learnt from bitter experience that the world was full of selfish people, and she had no desire to stake her hard-earned money on a dodgy scheme with no other assurance apart from hope.

At the same time, she wanted to do better—she wanted to buy a house. She was not sure about getting married yet, as she still had financial responsibilities towards her family.

> GETTING RICH IS A CHOICE, THOUGH IT ENTAILS TAKING SOME CHANCES.

Wouldn't it be good if she could buy a house and bring her mother and the rest of her family to Delhi?

But a house costs a lot. The concern occupying her night and day was how to plan her savings better in order to meet that goal.

She had no exposure to money management, financial planning or any financial understanding of investments and how they worked. As a child, she knew only that her uncle, who made Rs 25,000 per month as a bank clerk, was the best paid in her family and could afford a comfortable life for his family. That amount of Rs 25,000 and the good life it afforded had been the height of her ambition for so long, but now, the Rs 35,000 per month she made was just enough for her, even when she was staying in a dormitory in a working women's hostel, sharing a hall with three bathrooms with twenty other women.

She called her uncle and a few friends, all of whom gave her varied advice. This confused her further. One day, after work, she was very hungry and wanted to have bun maska and filter coffee. It was salary day, she was tired after a long day of work, and she felt like just sitting and eating in peace before returning to her hostel.

THE BIGGEST GIFT YOU CAN GIVE TO YOUR CHILD IS FINANCIAL LITERACY.

She ordered filter coffee and bun maska as she entered the Parsi Tea Shop. The menu card was lying on the table and all the other tables were full. She glanced through the menu and realized that the price of the filter coffee had moved from Rs 20 to Rs 30, and the bun maska would now cost her Rs 25 instead of the Rs 20 she had paid six months back. She went to the uncle at the counter and asked why these prices had gone up. The Parsi gentleman told her that everything had become more expensive thanks to inflation. He added that next month, he would have to increase the prices of all his items even further to manage his outgoings. Plus, the employees at the cafe were finding it difficult to manage with the meagre salaries he had been paying them so far. He would have to increase the salaries of his staff as well, and so the cost of bun maska would rise further.

Priya worried how she would manage her expenses if prices increased across the board—her salary been increasing by only 4-5 per cent every year, but her expenses seem to be jumping up rapidly. She did get a good rise of 20 per cent after her recent promotion, but her superior had made it quite clear that this was a one-off event and that she should not expect similar payouts each year. She was still puzzling over this when suddenly, a bearded man in a black half jacket with a national-flag pin shining on his upper pocket sat down in front of her. He ordered a filter coffee. Before Priya could say something, the man said, 'Apologies, madam, I have sat down in front of you uninvited as there are no other tables.'

Priya didn't say a word. The bearded man took a few phone calls and spoke to the callers politely about investing, patience, money, etc. That made Priya curious and she asked him about it. The man replied that people called him Gautam and that he helped people with their financial well-being. This sounded like jargon to her and she probed further. The man patiently replied to all her questions about money, savings, investing and success.

They spoke about the primary requirements of food, clothes, Wi-Fi or mobile networks and shelter, and about how these needs can be met if savings are channelled in the right direction.

Priya realized this was a godsend; she didn't wish to waste this opportunity. This was her ticket to change the class she was born into and fulfil her dream of buying a house.

Every society is stratified and most people who become powerful exploit that hierarchy to gain power. Some of these hierarchies are based on religion, some on caste, some on colour and some on knowledge, but the most common and natural stratification in modern society is based on money, economics, resources or financial prowess. They all mean the same.

When money is the basis of social stratification, people are classified into one of six categories:

i. Ultra rich
ii. Wealthy
iii. Upper middle class
iv. Middle class
v. Lower middle class
vi. Poor

These divisions are not discussed openly, they are not always acknowledged, but they form the most pervasive social barriers.

These categories are generally so watertight that movement from one to another can happen to the extent of a single step, upwards or downwards, but any further change is restrained.

Then there are preachers and masters who say *'Money isn't everything'*. But if this money is absent, everything in life can turn topsy-turvy. It is easy for people who have made it big in life to preach detachment.

Thus, the modified concept: **'Money isn't everything, but it's something that can assist one in attaining all one desires, at least materially.'**

As we know, deficit or excess of anything is harmful, but a moderate and minimum quantity of some things is essential for one's well-being, be it wealth, physical exercise or thinking.

Why is it essential to have a minimum threshold, what is that minimum threshold and how is it computed?

A minimum monetary threshold is essential for one's mental, physical and emotional well-being.

Humans are nothing but an outcome of the decisions they take. Decisions determine our future. We don't know the outcomes of our decisions and that's why life is interesting.

What influences one's decision-making?

Morals, values, experiences, people, exposure to literature, consumption of social media, books . . . in a nutshell, innumerable things influence us.

The most significant of them all is the environment one is exposed to.

A change in environment can lead to a change in thinking, change in perspective, and, subsequently, this leads to a different direction of decision-making.

Our environment can be an enabler or a deterrent. It propels one to use different parts of the body. Some environments lead to conflict and thus engender excess use of voice or words, some environments inspire one to think and, thus, aid the development of mental prowess. The environment, without a doubt, plays a significant role in how a person functions.

Humans are adaptable and their instinct is survival, A human being, therefore, adapts to a new environment to survive.

One common example of the influence of the environment on a person is the performance of the same person in similar roles in different organizations that have different cultures, respecting and propagating different values. One keeps hearing about these so-called turnaround stories, but what enables these turnarounds for people and organizations is the environment.

If the environment is so important, can it be quantified in monetary terms?

Abode, location of the abode and the neighbourhood make the difference. A struggling, unsanitary and conflict-filled neighbourhood not only hinders our well-being, but adversely affects decision-making abilities, thereby impacting our future.

It can be argued that we can always leave these worldly intricacies, nuances and complications and move to the Himalayas. But even to move to the Himalayas, one needs to have money. The flippant individual might say, 'You should renounce the world in its entirety and live as a monk', but that is difficult and seldom happens.

So what is that minimum monetary prowess one should have?

- ✓ A comfortable house in a comfortable neighbourhood where one wishes to spend the next couple of decades.
- ✓ Three years of monthly expenses invested in equities.
- ✓ Six months of emergency funds invested in short-term liquid debt.

How can one invest in equities?

If one wishes to jump more than one notch in the economic hierarchy or maintain one's place in the top notch, what should be done?

There are only three solutions to this:

1. *Start a business solving one of the big problems that presently exist on this planet.* Businesses can be of two types: solving local problems or solving global problems.

If one solves a problem that costs millions, one will attract funding in the millions; if one is solving a problem that affects billions, one will get funding in the billions. The bigger the problem, the bigger the chances of one becoming a billionaire.

2. **Join a start-up as a co-founding member or be part of the initial team.** You will get ESOPs (employee stock ownership plans) and they can become valuable if the business grows, but will drop to zilch in value if the business fails. The failure of a business will teach you essential lessons for the next job and if the business succeeds, you will find yourself moving up the socio-economic hierarchy.

3. **Invest in the intelligence of others who are scaling up their businesses in the listed market place.**

   With the third point comes a conundrum: in FY 2016, there were 4321 listed companies in India, removing the overlap between NSE and BSE. Despite having mega IPO years in 2021 and 2022, which saw the listing of 64 and around 125 companies respectively, the total number of companies in FY 2022 stood at 4534.[1] A limited number of companies willingly bought back their shares and delisted. Most just became defunct and died. In a tough year that sees rough weather in the financial markets, roughly two dozen IPOs come on to the main bourses and in a good year, the number of IPOs can range from forty to

---

[1] 'Number of companies listed in NSE and BSE across India FY 2008-2022', Statistica, 20 November 2023, available at https://www. statista.com/statistics/731969/india-number-of-companies-listed-in-nse-and-bse/#:~:text=In%20financial%20year%202022%2C%20a,-compared%20to%20the%20previous%20year.

one hundred.[2] Despite this, the number of businesses listed on the bourses remains about the same.

Hence, to protect what one has and grow from there, one needs a success formula for Indian equities.
This is called the 100X Formula.

<u>**What is this recipe for success?**</u>
Four pillars of 100X formula + 20 high-quality businesses screened through these pillars + 5-year holding period.
And returns are generated.

FIIs (Foreign Institutional Investors) or **FPIs (Foreign Portfolio Investors)** have known for decades that a country with favourable demographics (two-thirds of the population aged between fifteen and fifty-nine and one-third in the dependent age), accompanied by a large literate population, together with high aspirational demand, cannot remain slow for long periods.

Mixed with favourable governance and reforms, the outcome is positive, and thus growth in the underlying economy, as well as inflation, by and large on account of steady demand, will remain high.

In simpler words, India will never have nominal growth (real GDP + inflation) of less than a double-digit or a very high single-digit rate. If India grows, good companies' profitability in the country should beat the nominal Indian GDP in a four-to-five-year cycle of global boom and bust. Thus, investing in India and high-quality businesses is a no-brainer.

---

[2] 'List of IPOs by year in India (Mainboard IPO)', Chittorgarh, available at https://www.chittorgarh.com/report/list-of-ipo-by-year-fund-raised-success-mainboard/85/.

Why should large savings be channelled into equities?

The Case for Equities

Fortunately, or unfortunately, equity is the simplest and easiest way to multiply one's net worth.

All other asset classes, including gold, debt and real estate, in India deliver post-tax and post-inflation negative returns.

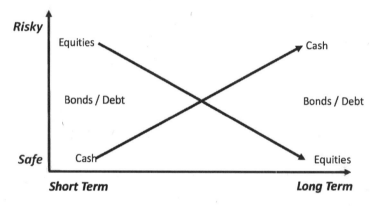

What's safe is short term is risky in long term

*Cash is risky in long term due inflation and positive interest rate
** Reinvestment is one of the major risks that is usually undermined while investing in debt

- ✓ **Debt:** Pre-tax generally matches up to inflation, and if one takes the higher risk to generate a few percentage points more debt returns, the credit risk increases manifold. In simpler terms, taking additional risks in debt can be tantamount to the loss of the entire principal as well.
- ✓ **Gold** makes money as the supply of gold is scarce. If chaos, calamity or catastrophe ever strikes, gold becomes the saviour and a natural medium of exchange or barter.

    Thus, every downturn in the economic, social or geopolitical environment brings an opportunity to make lots of money in gold. However, when fear, crisis or panic are at their peak, gold peaks as well. And when the mind is fearful, scared and filled with trepidation, the ability to think rationally and book profits ceases to exist.

> EVEN IF YOU BUY PURE GOLD AT DOUBLE THE PRICE NOW, YOU WILL EVENTUALLY MAKE MONEY . . . BUT WHEN?

When fear abates, gold prices also moderate, and thus the opportunity to make large amounts of money evaporates.

In the end, gold meets the pre-tax inflation returns over longer periods.

Basically, panic reduces the possibility of rich returns in gold.

✓ **Real Estate** is localized and returns depend on external activity being undertaken in the area. Real estate can give post-tax, post-inflation marginal positive returns, but again, investing in real estate can be skewed, lopsided and uneven. The challenges are liquidity (due to a wide bid and ask gap or a mismatch in demand and supply), low transparency (possibility of frauds) as well as significant time, money and energy costs in maintaining and dealing with real estate.

Beyond the real estate that is needed to maintain a high-quality life and lifestyle, anything more can create difficulties.

The maximum one can get from real estate is marginal returns. Real estate sees a massive jump every couple of years but remains stagnant for longer periods. One sees the returns from inception onwards and believes that one is making continuous money, but that money, once made, stops growing after a point.

Two essential factors leading to the above perplexity:

I. **Economics of real estate:** Real estate math is simple—one-third is land, one-third is construction cost and one-third is the margin of the developer. The interest cost sometimes, obviously, reduces the margin of the developer and sometimes, the developer perpetuates returns by selling the house pre-construction or under construction.

   The current cost of construction per square foot (carpet) in India is in the range of Rs 1000 to 2500 depending on quality, location, etc.[3] Now, if the land cost is between Rs 500 and 4500 per square foot, the final cost for the end user will come to between Rs 3500 and 13,500 per square foot.

   If one buys, compounding may occur at the rate of 14–15 per cent for next few years, but then it stagnates—the first 100 per cent jump is achieved quickly, but after that, the second doubling takes an almost impossibly long time to materialize.

   Thus, buying real estate is good and one should constantly upgrade one's property, but only for

---

[3] Multiple sources indicate costs ranging from Rs 2500 to 6000. As building materials and equipment for construction and labour have become more expensive, the costs mentioned here are estimates. See Jay N. Prasad, 'What's the Average Home Construction Cost in India?', Houseyog (available at https://www.houseyog.com/blog/whats-the-average-home-construction-cost-in-india/#:~:text=Today%2C%20average%20home%20construction%20cost%20can%20range%20between,of%20finish%20you%20want%20in%20your%20new%20house) and 'How We Can Construct A Home at A Low Cost In Mumbai 2022', Honest Broker, 29 February 2024 (available at https://www.honestbroker.in/blogs/How-We-Can-Construct-A-Home-at-A-Low-Cost-In-Mumbai#:~:text=Average%20Construction%20Cost%20In%20Mumbai,in%20Pune%20and%20Delhi%2C%20respectively).

consumption. Mixing real estate with investments is not a great idea.

II. **Instant depreciation in real estate:** As soon as one enters a real-estate transaction, one is down by about 12 per cent or sometimes even more—stamp duty alone is 6 to 7 per cent, depending on the city, 5 per cent (earlier 12 per cent) is the GST on under-construction property, 0.5 per cent or so is the registration cost, there is brokerage (if any) and the transfer fee to the society, plus the cost of doing up the interiors.

The contradiction of human behaviour is that when people buy real estate or property, they are okay with an immediate 10 or 15 or 20 per cent downside, but if the same happens to their financial investments due to macro or geopolitical reasons, they lose their calm. This kind of behaviour may be attributed to the fact that fluctuations in real-estate prices are not visible on a day-to-day basis, whereas one can see stock prices fluctuate on screen every day.

Thus, if one needs to break the shackles of economic stratification of society, ownership in a businesses is a must, either directly or indirectly, using any of the three methods mentioned above.

Time and timing are the greatest friends of riches. But the question on every investor's mind is: how much time to spend and how to time the investment?

The Science of Time to Be Spent and Timing the Market

Thanks to the Internet, Covid-19 and rapid digitization, financial knowledge has been democratized.

There is too much information available, with results and the analyses of results reaching the common man and the most astute fund managers in parallel.

The mistake that hurts the most!

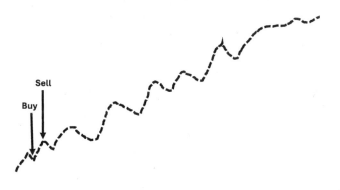

This begs the question, why do most people still fail to make a fortune in the stock markets when a few fund managers can?

The answer is simple: in equities, patience pays, and enduring patience coupled with a high emotional quotient pay handsomely.

Starting from the basics

Stock Price = EPS × PE (earnings per share X price to earnings ratio)

Let's understand why, even in good businesses, investors don't end up making money.

1. **Inconsistent EPS:** There are many businesses that are cyclical in nature, like businesses that are highly sensitive to government spending or interest rates or global commodity supercycle or crude prices. Some of these businesses are not able to pass on the increases in the prices of the underlying raw material due to intense competition or on account of fragmented markets or being a B2B player in

the middle of two behemoths (one large supplier for procuring raw material and one large customer for buying the end product manufactured by the company). Thus, if one buys these businesses at any point without understanding the macro supercycle of global events and ignoring the changes in the economic environment, then one may have to witness time-wise (stock price moves in a particular range for longer periods) or price-wise (stock price significantly corrects from the price one has bought and comes back to the same price after a significant period) corrections.

Solution: One needs to see two things—the past decade's macro supercycles, their longevity and impact, and the company or business's resilience in absorbing the downturn in the macro supercycle.

Both can be assessed by checking the diluted EPS for the last five to six years. If the EPS has been growing consistently at low or mid-double digits despite challenges in the global supercycle, one can proceed with the stock purchase.

2. **Stocks bought at higher PE (rich valuations)—the fallacy of one good quarter:** A few get swamped or swept away in the euphoria of equity markets, buying businesses at any valuation.

There is a common tendency in the equity markets—market participants rely on the last available information as the gospel truth and consider the word of the promoter or management final. Imagine a scenario in which a company has been delivering tepid numbers for successive quarters and then a bonanza quarter is delivered. The market takes into account the last quarter and starts building the possibilities of the future on that basis.

Furthermore, analysts start assessing the company and building estimates, and if the results are below the analysts' estimates, then the stock corrects. Lastly, great emphasis is placed on management commentary, but neither the management nor the analyst can predict sudden changes in the geopolitical or economic environment, and so buying on the basis of such factors can again lead to steep price corrections.

Long Term Investing in Bull Market Vs Bear Market

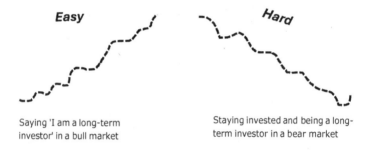

Saying 'I am a long-term investor' in a bull market

Staying invested and being a long-term investor in a bear market

The simple solution to this problem is figuring out the past median multiple of the company itself. The average range of the PE multiple over the past few years should be assessed and if the increase in the PE multiple is 20 to 30 per cent and is within the tolerance limit, then one can get into the business at that price.

3. **Predicting the future growth or prospects of the business:** This is the mother of all investment challenges—to predict the probability of success of the business. There are two major challenges for any business:

   I. **Utilization of free cash flows:** It's interesting that most businesses in India—thanks to demographics, demand and digitization—if conducted with reasonable smartness, reasonable acumen, reasonable risk and integrity, break even at the operating level in 1100 days and at the net profit level, taking into account all costs, in about 1850 days. The toughest time for a business is between days 180 and 540. Most businesses don't sustain that long. Once the 540th day passes, things start to improve and an upward trajectory begins. Some businesses are able to raise money sooner and sail through this tough period with ease.

After the 1850th day, when the business starts to throw free cash flows, what happens to that cash? Is it reinvested to grow the product range, gain market share, achieve mechanization to improve efficiency, invest in ancillary businesses or divergent businesses or increase the perks of the promoters? This decision determines the future of business. What's applicable to new businesses is also applicable to old businesses.

Can a Rs 500 crore turnover business scale up to Rs 5000 crore of business in the next seven to ten years? The answer lies in the capital allocation of free cash flows. Understanding this brings higher predictability of success and better chances of the growth of the business one is investing in.

> THE BASIC TENET OF A BUSINESS IS TO STOP BURNING CASH AS QUICKLY AS POSSIBLE.

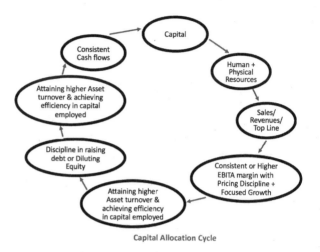

Capital Allocation Cycle

II. **Growing the business from a small one to the next level:** Whether a business can scale up from 500 crore to 5000 crore also depends upon the allocation of resources in the business. For growth, mindset is the key. Sometimes, external perspectives need to be introduced to the business when its mindsets needs transformation. If the promoter tightly controls and manages the business, the chances of scaling it up will be limited. External human resources having skin in the game and aligned with the interests of the company through equity (ESOP) ownership can, therefore, take the company to greater heights. There are numerous examples of visionary promoters who invested in the right talent pool, the right technology and the right processes to achieve phenomenal scale.

> EVENTUALLY, EQUITIES WILL ALWAYS WIN, AS THEY HAVE THE WISDOM, ALIGNMENT OF INTERESTS AND THE EXPERTISE OF MANY MORE PEOPLE THAN ANY OTHER ASSET CLASS.

The Making of Market Capitalization

Once invested, one should remain invested through the cycles for a period of at least sixty to seventy-two months. As markets are evolving, equity cycles are becoming shorter. It's always advisable to remain invested for at least two cycles of the market of thirty to thirty-six months each.

Often, investors wait for the dip or the bottom of the market. It is essential to note is that when investors use the word 'market', they mean the large cap index, i.e., Nifty or Sensex. Now, Sensex or Nifty correction may not mean correction or downturn in individual stocks and vice versa, unless one is investing purely in Nifty or Sensex MFs or ETFs.

Furthermore, as one remains invested for longer periods in businesses that are able to grow in a relatively linear manner in terms of revenues and earnings, such businesses keep multiplying their earnings and thus, with every passing day, the PE keeps becoming cheaper.

Once due diligence with regard to the business, its consistency and its relative valuation in comparison to its past is undertaken, one should move ahead with the investment.

The challenge with timing the market is that no one knows how long and how far the market correction will be and when the bounce-back will happen, as triggers are never predictable.

Thus, the time spent in the market is more important than timing the market. If one witnesses a black swan event, and when fear is at its peak, one should get in and shop aggressively in the market, else deploy investments consistently in a systematic and disciplined manner after doing due diligence on the business one wishes to own.

What's the right PE multiple to buy the business at?

Look at the past and the tolerance limit apart from future growth. **Check the PE and the past median PE.**

Should one compare PE multiples of the business with those of other companies in the same sector?

Can a marathon runner and a sprint runner be compared?

Does a small-cap company deserve a higher PE multiple due to higher growth in the same sector?

Isn't a small-cap company more susceptible to market challenges, margin shrinkage and customer concentration as compared to a large-cap company?

Simplifying Indian equity investing for anyone with Rs 5000 to Rs 50 crore or more

Some rules of equity investing:
- ✓ The first equity investment should always be in Nifty as Nifty is the composite index of the top fifty companies as per market capitalization and has a fantastic in-built system that automatically weeds out businesses that are slowing down.
- ✓ Money belongs to the investor and thus, the investor needs to invest time as well. The portfolio should be reviewed religiously, at least every quarter, and

monitored along with the advisor, if any, else by oneself. What can't be monitored and reviewed can't be corrected, what can't be corrected can't be changed, and what can't be changed will have the same outcome.

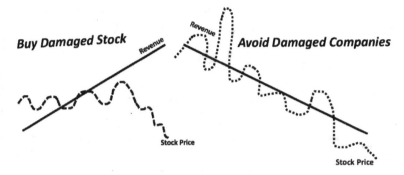

✓ Monitoring and review do not mean taking action, even if none is required. Review means taking stock of what and why.
✓ Due diligence should be conducted before investing, not after.
✓ While investing in a managed fund (mutual fund or PMS or AIF), one should look at the composition of the team and not just returns—the system, the framework, the process and the people.
✓ Hero worship, stardom and key man risk should be avoided in investing.

Investor Mindset – Pride Or Opportunity?

- ✓ Funds needed within twenty-four months should never form part of equity investing. Ideally, they should be invested for thirty-six to seventy-two months. Twenty-four months is just a gamble.
- ✓ In a span of forty-eight to fifty-four months, diluted EPS growth is reflected in the stock price growth, ignoring PE multiples to a large extent.
- ✓ Martin Luther King Jr said, 'If you can't fly then run, if you can't run then walk, if you can't walk then crawl, but whatever you do, you have to keep moving forward.' Similarly, for a bright, independent future in which one needn't work for money but for happiness and satisfaction, one should keep investing, if not every day, then every week, if not every week, every month, if not every month, then every quarter, but keep investing.
- ✓ If a lump sum is not available, invest through small systematic investment plans.
- ✓ Only withdraw money from equities when you are replacing equities with any other appreciating asset, not a depreciating asset.
- ✓ Too much fragmentation and too much concentration in portfolios are harmful. Don't put all your eggs in one basket, but also don't buy too many stocks or investments that can't be tracked.
- ✓ As the corpus grows, keep adding money to your winners and keep weeding out losers. Never cut the legs of your fastest horses.
- ✓ In life and in investments, continuity and consistency are key.

Missing the Multi-Bagger

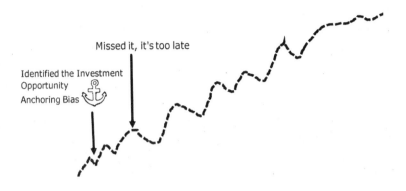

Abstract Yet Essential Traits Necessary to Win in Investing

Successful investors have written a lot about cognitive biases—some say ten, some say thirty and some say fifty. The list is long and can be looked up easily.

Most know about these biases but fall into the same traps anyway. We are wired to choose the easier path and our cognitive biases lead us to those traps, perceived shortcuts and quick fixes, to meet our challenges.

What can combat cognitive biases is muscle memory, or, simply put, habits.

Habits are the reasons why those very few who flourish realize their peak potential. Good habits, once formed, often save us and help us move ahead.

The formula for this is called **PCR Matrix.**

Patience: This seemingly simple attribute is actually fairly complex. Most believe the meaning of patience is the ability to wait. However, the key is the ability to wait without getting apprehensive, anxious or annoyed, yet keeping the goal in sight and continuing to prepare to reach it.

Patience is generally lost if there is a lack of information or information asymmetry. This is where due diligence and notes made during diligence come in handy. When the mind gets vulnerable with impatience, the notes remind one of their beliefs and convictions with which one started.

Almost all fund managers and investment houses have notes about investments, popularly called 'investment thesis'. The irony is that generally, no one looks at these when things start to go south. People start looking for the latest piece of information, which then supersedes all prior knowledge gathered.

This is how the world works—the last quarterly results, the last performance of the sportsperson and last month's achievement of the salesperson determine people's immediate behaviour towards it.

This brings us to the second point.

Cutting the noise: In the 5G world, information, misinformation, facts, fake facts, perceptions and impressions are aplenty. Two experts from the same field can form diametrically opposite viewpoints from the same data, exactly the way there is a buyer and there is a seller at the same price in the stock market, both having exactly opposite viewpoints on the same business at a particular point.

> VALUE, GROWTH, SPECIAL SITUATIONS, ETC. ARE ONLY SEMANTICS— EVERYTHING WILL MAKE MONEY AT A PRICE AND WITH PATIENCE.

Too much noise leads to fogging in the mind and thus to muddled decisions. This cannot be emphasized enough—due diligence on the business, valuation, ecosystem and moats should be conducted before putting your money in, not after the investment has been made.

When too much uncertainty prevails, accompanied by too much noise, go back to the basics—basic business model and cash flows. When it comes to investing, the resilience of mind is equally, if not more, important as the resilience of the business one is investing in. As the equity markets go through volatile periods, one should have the capacity to withstand tough situations and ignore unnecessary noise emerging from factors extraneous to the business. If the business is robust and its fundamentals are sound, an investor must not worry about short-term market fluctuations. Every investment goes through volatility, and those who stand steady when everyone is flustered and fearful usually emerge victorious and inspire others. Thus last behavioural trait is remaining resilient when the going gets tough.

A few other tips one should remember while investing are:

- ✓ Boring is beautiful: A lot of excitement and constant changes can be detrimental to the growth of the business and free cash flows. The businesses that try to capture every new opportunity in unrelated spaces finally end up misallocating capital and that will lead to the downfall of the firm.
- ✓ Cutting/reducing costs: Costs are certain while growth, income or revenue from the investment is uncertain. Thus, costs certainly will compound while returns or income may or may not compound. Cutting and reducing costs by every paise matters to ensure compounding.
- ✓ Churn is costly: Churn means buying and selling stocks frequently. Churn entails regulatory costs, heightened taxability, intermediation costs and brokerage cost, and so heavy churn can be expensive and can harm the investment.
- ✓ Go beyond the obvious and dig deeper for why and what: The numbers and data are known to

every analyst. Dig deeper into how motivated the management and promoter are to grow the business. Often, the businesses one owns in the portfolio are those whose products one uses. While buying the product or using the services, our experience as a customer or in dealing with the retail outlet or retailer of the product provides an understanding of what the future of the business looks like.

✓ Capitalizing on irrational mispricing of markets: Markets or sectors often provide opportunities where mega bucks can be made through irrational oversold positions due to the macro supercycle or international business ups and downs or global sector rotation. As a result, getting into a business when it is dirt cheap due to extraneous factors can be handsomely rewarding.

✓ Avoiding herd mentality: A herd generally chases the same thing when many receive the same information, and the popular perception is that nothing can go wrong. People join the bandwagon only when a large portion of the gains are no longer available. So, never chase momentum. Be wise and don't fall into this trap.

✓ Neither greedy, nor fearful, neither pessimistic, nor overly enthusiastic, just optimistic—more money is made on the long side than on the short side. Growth, positivity and a favourable outlook are always helpful.

✓ Don't get married to losers. Cut the losses, cut the umbilical cord. Capital always has a cost. If the capital has no cost, then there is an opportunity cost. Mistakes are bound to happen, but cutting losses and moving on is the hallmark of a successful investor.

Investing and Investment Outcomes Trick the Mind

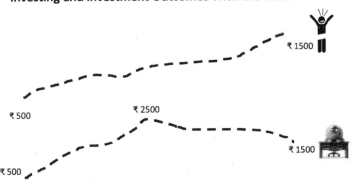

₹ 500

₹ 2500

₹ 500

₹ 1500

₹ 1500

✓ Taking a higher risk doesn't guarantee higher returns. There are two kinds of risks in the market: systematic risk and systemic risk. The systematic risk is the market risk and is difficult to predict, but the systemic risk is a company or business-specific risk that can be estimated to a large extent from the company's history and trajectory. The simplest way of reducing systematic risk is having a longer holding capacity during longer periods of uncertainty by keeping a certain amount of capital in the safety pockets.

✓ Predicting the cash flows and earnings trajectory is the key, not predicting the stock price. A successful investor is able to gauge earnings and the earnings growth trajectory with reasonable accuracy. Even if the guess is not entirely accurate, money will be made if the direction and trajectory are correct.

> CASH IS REAL, THE REST CAN ALL BE COOKED UP.

The Formula

Most investors focus either on cash flows or future earnings growth. This formula enables both.

The four parts of the formula are:

i.　CFOT1 > CFOT0
ii.　CFO/EBIT > 60 per cent
iii.　EBT/Total Capital Employed > 12 per cent
iv.　When to invest with nearly 100 per cent probability of winning—Trailing Year CFO/Current Market Cap > 15 per cent

The first three work on ascertaining the certainty of EPS growth and the last one on the PE or valuations.

The first three formulas need to be checked for the last five full year numbers and then one waits for the valuation during the year, allocating 5 per cent of the capital to every stock, and sticking to a maximum of twenty stocks.

Knocking out debris using the first formula enables us to remove the dregs of the markets. Then the second formula is applied and then the third. Once the business selection is ascertained, all there is left to do is being patient and vigilant.

The correctly priced business will certainly be picked at the opportune time.

The 100x formula uses a simple structure with four quality, straightforward checks for investments to identify twenty high quality stocks with equal weights, and then requires leaving the portfolio for five years. It is a time-tested strategy as data shows that historically a portfolio constructed through this strategy not only outperformed the benchmark consistently, but also delivered healthy absolute returns, particularly when the broader markets experienced stress.

Before we describe the returns delivered by the 100x portfolio, let's explain the simple investment filters employed. To begin, out of the approximately 5000 listed companies in India, we will limit ourselves to the those with a minimum market capitalization of Rs 100 crore, which is around 1500–2000. Then, we look for companies which, over the previous five years, have grown the cash flow from operations year on year (YoY) consistently, while also generating a profit before tax/capital employed greater than 12 per cent, which we believe is the true picture of the return on capital employed (RoCE). We have not considered EBIT because interest payments are one kind of fixed cost which is already committed and cannot be considered for the RoCE. We also have quality profit checks, which is a CFO/EBIT greater than 60 per cent for the past five years. But, despite conducting the above quality checks, we can't create wealth without having a great margin of safety. Also, cash flow from operating activities (CFO)/market cap should be greater than 15 per cent, which means a payback period of six to seven years.

Consistency in Growth (CFOT1 > CFOT0)

The CFO represents the amount of cash generated from core business activities such as manufacturing and selling goods, services, etc. Operating activities include revenue generation, payment of expenses and working capital funding. Generally, CFO is calculated using net income, non-cash items and changes in working capital.

$$\text{CFO} = \text{Net income} + \text{Non-cash items} + \text{Changes in working capital}$$

We believe cash generation is more important than revenue generation. The growth in cash generation indicates the company is growing and producing healthy cash flows. Our formula suggests that the current year's cash flow from operations (CFO1) should be greater than last year's cash flow operations (CFO0). It shows that the company has generated healthy cash flows compared to last year. This parameter focuses on cash flows instead of revenue.

Simply, CFOT1 > CFO0 indicates consistency in cash flows.

For this to be true three things should happen:

1. Revenue should grow.
2. Cost should come down.
3. Payments and receivables should be in control or decreasing in nature.

We hold the belief that if CFO has demonstrated growth over the past five years, it reflects diligent management efforts in driving business success. Remarkably, this simple formula filters out approximately 50 per cent of companies from our extensive list of 1500–2000 candidates.

Quality of Growth (CFO/EBIT > 60 per cent)

Earnings before interest and tax (EBIT) indicates the company's profitability. EBIT ignores the tax burden and capital structures and focuses on the company's ability to generate revenue from operations. EBIT helps identify those companies generating revenue to pay off interest/debt obligations and funding ongoing operations. EBIT can be calculated in two ways—one is revenue minus expense, excluding interest and tax, and another way is adding net income to interest and tax.

$$\text{EBIT} = \text{Revenue} - \text{Cost of goods sold (COGS)} - \text{Operating expenses}$$

EBIT = Net income or Profit after tax (PAT) +
Interest + Taxes

CFO/EBIT indicates how much cash flow is generated from the company's profitability. EBIT is the indicator of the company's profitability. The company should generate more than 60 per cent of its cash flows from profitability. If CFO/EBIT is more than 60 per cent, that means that the company has converted more than 60 per cent of EBIT into cash. For example, the cash profit should be more than 60 per cent for every one rupee of EBIT. The reason why we believe 60 per cent is optimal as one has seen that at least 40 per cent of EBIT gets stuck in working capital which is also called operating expenditure (Opex).

In our experience, we feel that some businesses need at least 40 per cent of EBIT to be earmarked for their receivables, inventories and payables, which lets the business generate, at a minimum, 60 per cent in cash profits.

If the formula holds, it means the company effectively transforms its accrued profits into tangible cash flow, ensuring financial stability. Maintaining a cash conversion rate of at least 60 per cent is crucial for operational readiness, especially in addressing unforeseen expenses or emergencies.

Let's break down a simple analogy: Imagine running a local coffee shop where you sell 100 cups a day at Rs 10 each, generating Rs 1000 daily. With no credit sales or purchases, and inventory managed just-in-time, your EBIT (earnings before interest and taxes) aligns perfectly with your CFO (cash flow from operations). It's akin to seeing a reflection in a mirror—both EBIT and CFO mirror each other when depreciation is disregarded.

Consider this: If CFO1 surpasses CFO0, it indicates growth. Similarly, if CFO divided by EBIT exceeds 60 per cent consistently over five years, it signifies a stronger base at every interval, affirming growth in EBIT. For the formula to hold true, CFO should continue to grow or remain higher than the previous figure, creating a continuous cycle of growth, akin to a circular motion.

Efficiency in Growth

Earning before tax indicates the company's profitability without considering tax expenses, or how much a company earns without factoring in taxes. EBT is calculated using operating and non-operating incomes. EBT is calculated by EBIT minus interest expense. It's calculated in another way too: net income plus taxes.

$$EBT = EBIT - Interest\ expense$$
$$EBT = Net\ income + Taxes$$

Capital employed refers to the capital utilized to generate profits. The capital comprises debt and equity. The total capital employed comprises total debt and total equity, or the sources of funds. Capital employed is total equity plus long-term liability. It's also calculated in another way: total assets minus current liabilities.

$$Capital\ Employed = Total\ Equity + Long\text{-}Term\ Liabilities$$

Equity is a liability for the company and an asset for investors. Equity essentially represents funds that the company owes to its owners and shareholders.

Long-term liabilities are also called long-term debt. The company borrows money from banks or raises money from investors through debt instruments in order to run or expand the business. The company should pay interest for the long-term debt, which appears as an interest cost item in the profit and loss statement.

Our formula suggests that the company should earn more than 12 per cent of profits for its capital employed for the year.

EBT/Total Capital Employed > 12 per cent

If all of the above parameters are satisfied for at least five years, those companies can be selected for your portfolio.

Why EBT/Total Capital Employed > 12 per cent

In India, the long-term inflation rate is around 6 per cent and the long-term growth rate is around 6 per cent. Considering inflation rate and growth rate, the company should generate a bare minimum of 12 per cent EBT from its employed capital.

Valuation or Price for Growth

Trailing Year CFO/Market Cap > 15 per cent

Market capitalization indicates the total market value of all outstanding shares and the size of the company. It can be calculated using the share price and the number of outstanding shares.

$$\text{Market capitalization} = \text{Share price} * \text{Number of outstanding shares}$$

Markets are unpredictable and we may not always be able to time them. Our formula suggests that the cash flows generated from the business for each rupee of the market cap indicate how fast the business recovers its market cap by the cash flows it generates.

CFO/Market capitalization > 15 per cent

For example, if the market cap is Rs 100 and the cash flow from operations is Rs 15, it tells us that the business can generate cash flows equivalent to the invested market cap in 6.6 years. This shows that the business has the potential to double in 6.6 years.

Investing in a business that has demonstrated consistent growth over the past five years and one that operates efficiently provides confidence in its ability to sustain growth in the future. Even with a modest 1 per cent growth annually, the payback period reduces, and higher growth further accelerates returns. Buying at a low valuation with growth potential ensures long-term capital preservation, with a payback period as low as 6.6 to 7 years. However, it's essential to validate this valuation approach by satisfying other key parameters over the same period and waiting for the right entry point that's 15 per cent > or = CFO/Market capitalization.

Why the 100X Formula Works

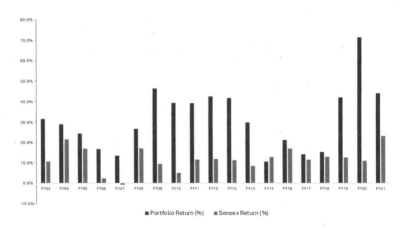

The 100X Strategy (the Ultimate Instrument of Wealth Creation)

For most Indians, investment means buying gold, land and real estate. The middle class, especially, has a strong affinity for gold as an investment. A lack of financial literacy prevents most people from managing their money smartly and growing it. Even the education system does not include financial literacy in any significant way—it is all oriented towards engineering, technology and science. Even those who study finance end up simply earning a salary and investing it in fixed deposits, gold and real estate.

Fixed deposits or FDs are the best alternative to gold, land and real estate for Indians. Most people are vehemently in favour of FDs in which, they believe, they can make a lot of money. They are thus surprised to discover that the bank only insures the first 5 lakh (DICGC) in FDs. In real estate and gold, the insurance is that these asset classes are tangible and have physical form. The stock market cannot be touched and felt for assurance and so people think it is risky—it is this misconception that makes people wary of investing in it.

In reality, the asset class that has really created wealth in any country is the markets.

If someone had invested Rs 1 lakh in the Sensex in 1998, it would have grown at a CAGR of 13.7 per cent to Rs 19.3 lakh from 1998 to 2022, while other asset classes grew at lower than 10 per cent CAGR in the same period.

> LEARN, AND TEACH YOUR CHILDREN ABOUT APPRECIATING AND DEPRECIATING ASSETS. THE SOONER THEY LEARN, THE LOWER THE CHANCES OF THEM DYING POOR.

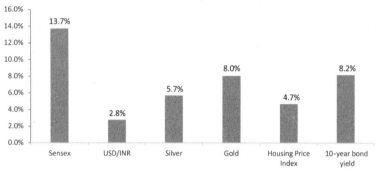

Most people who have grown up to adulthood in the past few decades have not lived life by their own wits. They live as per society's expectations. They buy homes, cars and expensive phones to show off. The smartest people take decisions wisely and they never buy expensive things to impress others.

4 Pillars of 100X Growth

Starting early, even with the smallest amount, leads to unbelievable benefits.

Less time means more panic, more churn, more mistakes— the later one starts the investing journey, the more returns one needs to generate to meet the end goal.

If a person who needs Rs 10 crore as a retirement corpus at the age of sixty starts investing at the age of fifty-five, they would need to save and invest a whopping Rs **10 lakh per month** for the next five years and the money would have to compound post-expenses, post-tax at the rate of **nearly 19** per cent.

On the other hand, by saving just Rs 6,000 per month for thirty years, and if one's wealth compounds at about 19 per cent, one can comfortably achieve a corpus of over Rs 10 crore.

It is true that 19 per cent is too ambitious considering that Nifty or Sensex, including dividends and corporate action, compounds at about 14 per cent over longer periods. Thus, even if one consistently, and in a disciplined manner, keeps investing Rs 18,000 per month just into Nifty, the corpus will hit the Rs 10 crore mark.

This is common knowledge; even an Excel formula can compute it easily.

What is not known or not realized is the elasticity of expenses and the inelasticity of income—income increases at a slower rate than expenses.

In middle age, when that person gets married and plans to start a family, expenses multiply while income remains the same, with lower chances of a significant jump, as time needs to be divided between family and work.

On the other hand, when a person is single, they have more time in hand to work, and work hard, to get bonuses and incentives and with relatively lower expenses. Thus, if one builds the habit of saving and investing from a young age, the rest of life will turn out to be relatively easier.

The habit of having an appreciating asset or a depreciating asset

As businesses grow, owners and employees both make more money through bonuses and salary hikes, but these bonuses and salary hikes usually lead to higher expenditure than a rise in sporadic or windfall income.

When there is a windfall income, the tendency is to buy a depreciating asset like a vehicle or spend on discretionary items, which only results in incremental expense for today and for the future as well.

A simple example is purchasing a high-end car with a bonus. One is comfortable with the car one is using but due to this windfall, one upgrades the car and buys and expensive one. The new car exhausts all potential savings and investments that could have led to the growth of the corpus, and wear and tear and repair in case of accidents or damage mean that the future expenses are also poised to jump, thereby reducing the percentage of savings further.

Another common example is getting the walls of one's house covered in fancy wallpaper. The walls of the house are in good condition, but remain the same in colour and appearance. The wallpapering is more to have something new and exciting in the décor than for any utility. The wallpaper peels off after a year or so, need to be replaced and are four or five times more expensive than painting the house. This one-time expense, made for 'status', becomes a recurring expense of the future.

Once the habit of overspending sets in, shedding it becomes a challenge and is a very painful process that is connected with the psychological concept of deprivation.

Thus, the elasticity of expenses is always higher while income is relatively inelastic. So a jump in income should never mean a jump in expenses. On the contrary, a jump in income should mean increase in savings and investments.

It was late evening when Gautam left the cafe. Priya had a long meaningful conversation with him. Gautam helped her understand the basics of investing and advised her to start investing early for a happy and purposeful life. Although it was too much for Priya to absorb, the conversation left her enriched, and she was now ready to start her journey of transformation from rags to riches.

5

Breaking the Corporate Curse

The quest to break the glass ceiling

Priya's journey of investing had begun. Her monetary ambitions were not for herself but for her mother and her family, who had struggled so that Priya could move out of the small village and their scraping, desperate life to the big city and make something more of herself. The family had not only enabled and encouraged her but also had emboldened her spirits, and that's why she was here, fighting to find her place, her corner in this land of hope where dreams did come true.

Whenever she faced difficulties, her family, her friends from the village and her mother inspired her and motivated her to overcome her despair. In return, she wanted to make her family feel proud of her. She did not face her struggles alone—her family faced, fought and confronted them with her daily and she wanted to put an end to the desperation and hopelessness of poverty for them.

Supercycle of Support

When a person stitches together a dream for themselves, wanting to change the status quo, challenging the common perception of 'can't be done', and on the journey they stumble, fall and suffer setbacks, they might sometimes give up and stay down, with no energy to get up. It is then that the family comes to the rescue—not physically or financially but emotionally and spiritually, supporting and encouraging the traveller to stand up and continue, since the worst is about to end.

FAMILY MATTERS, AND DURING TOUGH TIMES, FAMILY MATTERS EVEN MORE.

An unshakeable bond between oneself and the family can become the wind under one's wings, allowing them to achieve anything and everything in life.

Priya's case was similar. She wanted to do more and do well, not for herself but for her family, who had borne hardships so that Priya could get out and fly high.

Priya realized that investing would help, but saving from the meagre salary she drew was a challenge. She adopted financial discipline but the savings were minuscule and she needed to save more. But to save more, she needed to earn more.

How to do that?

Is working hard, persevering and burning the midnight oil the answer?

When one is starting one's career, hard work, dedication and going that extra mile each time can really make a difference.

But do the skills and attitude that got you the job also ensure that you rise in your company or move ahead on the corporate roller coaster?

The obvious answer is no.

What brought you here will not necessarily take you up there.

One must continue to polish, hone and sharpen their skills and add new ones, if one wishes to grow.

Seniors' Silent Expectations

> ASK AND PEOPLE
> WILL REPLY,
> MAKE MISTAKES
> AND PEOPLE
> WILL PUNISH.

These are the expectations of the corporate world or the unsaid rules of success. Most seniors expect these, but no one says so explicitly.

What is amusing is that as one moves upward from one bracket to another as defined in the graph, the subconscious mind craves the next element that has not been accomplished yet. However, the conscious mind continues to want more of what has already been achieved.

This is the biggest disconnect between the people who own corporate structures or are at the helm of the corporate hierarchy and the ones who are working hard in the corporate setup to rise to the top.

Let's dig deeper to analyse the disconnect between those who seek delivery of superior results and those who are expected to deliver, week on week, month on month, quarter on quarter, year on year and decade on decade.

Before digging vertically, let's start with the basics— what is the root of the problem and why is it critical to address it at the beginning?

What is capitalism (the basis of all businesses and corporations) and what does it focus on?

The system in which the free market regulates the demand and supply of goods and services, and capital chases the opportunity to maximize its returns. In other words, capitalism is an economic system in which the means of production or businesses are owned and run for profit by individuals.

The key here is the **maximization of profits or returns on the capital invested** and the focus perpetually remains the same, irrespective of the period or time frame.

Capitalism in its most granular form ignores the way those profits are gained, as long as it complies with the law of the land and doesn't get stuck in disputes or litigation. If disputes or litigation enhance the return on capital, then even they are perceived as a valuable strategy.

__Presumption__: Capitalism presumes that if maximizing one's gains at any cost was not suitable for a few or more, the marketplace would have discarded it, the profits would have declined and an equilibrium would be maintained.

However, it ignores the fact that as the market identifies unsuitable practices and prepares to discard them, the correction can be undercut by **greasing the system.** From a capitalist perspective, the system of greasing is a technique to ensure that the system runs well and smoothly. If any complication threatens a disruption, the oiling and greasing is increased to maintain the functioning of the system, restricting any upheaval. **Thus, in the capitalist system, this oiling and greasing is seen as an investment rather than as a leakage or wasteful expenditure.**

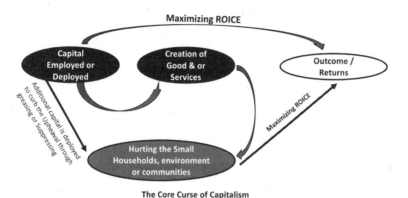

The Core Curse of Capitalism

Illustrating this through an ex.ample:

The Hunger for Annuity Income

The universe has created a human body with intellect, emotions and awareness. With its superior intellect, the ability to manage its emotions and its self-awareness, the human race ranks highest in the hierarchy of species on the planet. Additionally, the human species' power to take decisions, their ability to make choices from among various options and their ability to heal themselves makes them unique.

The body has an unquestionably excellent system of food intake and digestion and a similar process of extracting energy and nutrients from it for the body to heal and refuel itself.

No matter what food we eat, we need energy to digest it as well.

If we keep eating food throughout the day, the energy we could have used to do other constructive tasks is used to burn food inside the body. Thus, even after eating enough, or overeating a little or a lot, one feels sluggish, slack and lethargic rather than energetic.

Food is one of the biggest industries in the world—among the top seven globally. Despite significant human advancement, technological innovation and all the associated tricks and trickery, millions go hungry, millions waste excessive portions and an even larger number of humans fall ill due to excessive intake of food.

The food industry globally induces a habit of eating constantly and this constant eating or overeating leads to ailments, illness and sickness.

It goes against instinct to eat too much or to eat constantly, and this can be proven by a simple fact—when one falls ill on account of any ailment or experiences a symptom, like cough, cold, fever, nausea, running nose, congestion, aches and pains, the appetite drops immediately and the body's temperature rises.

The body raises its temperature to kill the infection and reduces the appetite so that low or no food intake will conserve the body's energy to heal and kill the foreign elements present rather than burning food in the process of digestion. Furthermore, every stream of medicine advises eating light food only and not heavy food in an illness, as it knows that the energy required to digest heavy foods will exacerbate the ailment rather than cure it.

Constant overeating leads to ailments, and so healthcare and pharmaceuticals are even bigger industries than food. The food industry supplies clients to the healthcare and pharma industries. The healthcare industry then suggests eating nutritious food along with medicines. The food industry then replaces the commonly used processed foods with whole foods, which contain no or little added sugars, flavours and other artificial ingredients, and escalates the price five to ten times. And the cycle continues.

Additionally, one knows that the body has a mechanism of self-healing, but the medicines prescribed suppress the symptom rather than curing the root cause of the ailment.

Furthermore, every allopathic medicine has side effects and thus, even if one ailment is cured, another develops. Thus, the patient remains a client for one or the other pharmaceutical company forever.

- Most blood pressure medications lead to an increase in blood sugar levels, leading to Type 2 diabetes.
- Cholesterol medications can lead to liver issues.
- Painkillers, which people pop casually and often, can lead to cardiovascular problems, heart ailments and other diseases.

Most doctors speak about the benefits rather than the risks while prescribing medication for the symptoms, since the patient as well as the doctor are looking for quick fixes.

> ETHICS ARE RARE, CHASING FOR GROWTH IS WIDESPREAD. STAND UP AND STAND OUT WITH ETHICS.

For generations, the sciences of Ayurveda, homoeopathy and chiropractic medicine have cured people, but these are not encouraged since, over time, these target the root cause and heal the body from within, leaving the patient with no reason to return and spend more money. However, modern medicine or allopathy promises an annuity income since it does not cure a disease but merely manages it. Essentially, it means that pharma companies continue to make money year after year as patients regularly need medicines to manage their diseases. The medicines often create side effects that need managing with more medication, ensuring that even as one ailment is cured, another emerges.

Growth in annuity income constantly and consistently means higher PE multiples for the business and thus, higher market capitalization.

Recalling a conversation between a venture capitalist and a biotechnology scientist:

The signs of bronchitis and asthma start with an allergy to certain things and lead to breathlessness and wheezing caused by certain triggers. These triggers can be air quality, pollutants or even pollen, dust and even high levels of stress or agitation. This is the body's signal that foreign particles entering the body have more potency than the body's power to fight foreign elements and infections.

Another common reason for wheezing is overeating. When one overeats, one feels uneasy and then it causes breathlessness and wheezing. For this complaint, most medical practitioners prescribe the drugs approved by the relevant Food and Drug Administration (FDA), and that includes steroids.

These give instant relief, but they don't remove the problem at the core and when the next trigger arises, immediate intervention has to be initiated again.

This biotechnologist developed a medicine containing a modified molecule which would stop the emergence of the allergy again as the molecule would help the body itself build antibodies to fight the allergy. A financial wizard developed a brilliant business plan and after initial patenting, submitted it to the venture capitalist.

Venture capitalists are clever and they know what might work and what is likely to fail through years of experience. This VC rejected this research and the proposal to develop it commercially.

The biotechnologist reworked the calculations and checked past data and records, but couldn't find any reason for the rejection. To his mind, it seemed that if the product were launched, it would be a hit as it would remove the ailment completely and almost permanently. It would benefit millions of people who would be free of the debilitating effects of the ailment, with very few side effects.

He requested a meeting with the VC and after many follow-ups, the venture capitalist agreed to meet on a Sunday. Their conversations went on for hours and covered everything, from the industry to climate change, humanity, etc. Finally, when the biotechnologist couldn't resist his impatience, he asked the senior partner at the VC firm the reason for the rejection.

The VC looked him in the eye and said that his invention and his drug didn't make business sense.

The biotechnologist opened his laptop, showed the VC the business plan and reeled off the numbers of even the most pessimistic projections of sales, which valued the drug alone at half a billion dollars in the next three to four years.

The venture capitalist replied, 'Your drug cures bronchitis or asthma from the root and in the shortest span of time. Also, the product includes instructions for how one should take this drug, which entail lifestyle changes and corrections in habits. Humans want quick fixes and that too without any effort, and so we need a drug that can provide a quick solution, but the ailment should re-emerge so that we can have repeat sales, increasing the annuity income.

'Furthermore, if this drug can cause harm to any other part of the body or any other internal or external organs, then we can ink income sharing contracts with other drug manufacturing companies for the enhanced sales of those additional medicines, which will push their sales higher.'

The VC went on to say that most drugs that treat bronchitis or asthma instantly if taken constantly may lead to increased pressure in the eyes, reduced bone density or fungal infections of the mouth. Thus, treatments to cure these secondary diseases yield more revenues and thus more profit to the firm.

The unfortunate reality of the world is that capitalism and business are perceived to be synonymous. However, one doesn't understand that a lopsided approach to business, which favours profit maximization rather than positive social impact, can lead to conflicts, and that can harm the existence of business altogether.

The Sanatana Solution

Sanatana's solution for this conundrum is to have the Ekatmik approach. It simply means that all elements are conjoint.

For centuries, Bharat has looked at an coexistence as Ekatmik, whether it pertains to plants, animals or any other part of the ecology. Everything from humans to mountains and rivers, from oceans to minerals embedded deep in the bedrock of the earth or sea, are all conjoint and part of the super macro manifestation of the universe. Super macro connection means everything on this planet and in the universe, including humans, plants, animals, planets and stars are interconnected. Thus nothing, absolutely nothing exists in isolation including luck, destiny, hard work, relationships or money.

Taking this concept further, super macro manifestation suggests that when one desires favourable outcomes for oneself, it's not just one aspect that needs changing. In fact, for something to turn favourable, a lot of elements in the universe collude to bring that positive change.

Hence, if one seeks favourable outcomes for oneself with a selfish mindset, then the results and repercussions can be grave. This has been the Vedic philosophy of Bharat. It further says that harm to any part of the ecology is bound to have an impact on human lives sooner or later.

This unsaid rule of sharing has also been mentioned in a short story mentioned in Vedic scriptures. Once, Goddess

Parvathi made laddoos for her son Lord Ganesha, who loved them. Lord Shiva was passing by, saw the laddoos and enquired about them. Goddess Parvathi told him that they were for Lord Ganesha. Lord Shiva asked if they could be given to his Ganas and Bhutas. She replied that the laddoos in the basket were few in number and would be insufficient. Lord Shiva said, 'You start offering them, they will not fall short.'

Goddess Parvathi started distributing the laddoos to the Ganas and the laddoos kept multiplying in the basket she was carrying. She distributed them to everyone in Kailasha and there were still laddoos left for Ganesha.

The unsaid rule of the planet is that one who shares, one who gives and one who helps always gets.

Despite ills, heightened materialism and fierce capitalism, businesses in the United States prosper because of equity sharing or the ESOP culture, which helps alignment of interests, brings focus and most importantly, engenders a sense of belonging and loyalty.

Despite extensive dilution in the early rounds, mammoth unicorns are created as everyone wins if the business wins.

Most promoter-led or majority promoter-owned businesses fail to grow or achieve their full potential despite having huge resources, the ability to buy or adapt new technology and the ability to buy superior talent. This can be attributed to this single cause: *'one who shares, one who gives and one who helps always gets it back multiplied.'*

Circling back to what it is that humans do not get despite being in the corporate culture and environment— what do they need?

Post-Covid, most organizations take a balanced approach to work, with work-from-home, work-life-leisure balance, performance-based pay scales and bonuses, and amenities like gymnasiums, sports, entertainment, food, cafeteria services, creches and others at the workplace. Still, attrition remains high.

The needs and the expectations of employees at different times within the corporate pyramid (*hierarchy in the corporate world*), are different. Also, there is always an expectation mismatch between the organization's owners and its employees. This gap is the biggest cause of stress for both owners and employees.

Much has been written about the culture of organizations and how culture influences the performance of individuals in the organization. Everyone wants a compassionate, empathetic, team-oriented culture, but when businesses have to deliver quarter-on-quarter numbers with millions of eyeballs on the quarterly performance, this conflict, clash or conundrum begs the question:

What is more important—**quarterly performance or a process to create clarity and consistency?**

COMMUNICATION AND A COMPASSIONATE ATTITUDE ARE FUTURE-PROOF SKILLS.

Furthermore, even if the corporate culture is compassionate and empathetic, meritocracy might sometimes take a back seat and the best talent leaves, frustrated at not being recognized for their superior output—they usually have options available since the competition always keeps a keen eye on superior performers.

Organizations that claim to balance compassion and meritocracy ensure that people are supported, but, at the same time, make sure that the bottom 10 per cent of their employees are moved out (in corporate language, 'weeded out') every year so that a balance is maintained. Unfortunately, in organizations that adopt this so-called balanced strategy, the employees also think in terms of a year-to-year appraisal cycle and thus, both organization and employees are unable to focus on longevity and miss out on the mutual benefits of a long-term association.

What is the solution?

Most believe the answer to this riddle is **'purpose'**.

What's the purpose of life?

Most say that once one finds their purpose, the drive to execute enhances and as drive and focus are sharpened, conquering anything becomes easier.

Unfortunately, as nothing is constant, a person's purpose also changes as they evolve, as the situation changes and as age catches up.

One only thinks about one's purpose in life when the basic needs of money, wellness and recognition are met. In Maslow's hierarchy of needs, purpose is the 'self-actualization' need, or the last need of the human. However, till the time one reaches their purpose in life, they still must work and deliver for their organization. Since the organization one works for also must make money to survive, it is essential that one continues to fulfil their professional responsibility while simultaneously finding their life's purpose.

What helps in this case—Contribution and Communication

The Key to Employee Retention and Employee Longevity

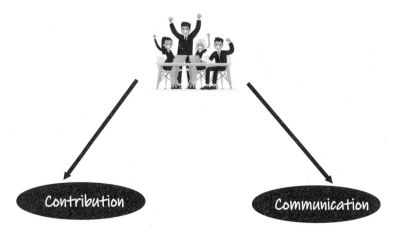

Contribution

What employees are looking for is their contribution to the overall scheme of things. In simple terms, is their work meaningful for the organization?

Is it creating an impact on the various stakeholders and is it enabling and helping the corporation to grow and gain its market share, reputation and social status?

One understands that even the smallest of actions by any and every employee has a butterfly effect.

A Short Story of the Butterfly Effect

Snippets from history

On 28 June 1914, Franz Ferdinand, Archduke of Austria, and Sophie, Duchess of Hohenberg, rulers of Austria-Hungary, were travelling in a motorcade to address the town hall at Sarajevo. An assassin hurled a bomb on Ferdinand's car. The bomb bounced off the car and exploded in the next car, wounding twenty people. Franz and Sophie, unhurt, reached the town hall, and addressed the crowd waiting for them.

After the town hall, Franz and Sophie decided to cancel the next stop on their programme and instead head to the city hospital to see the wounded. This time, they took a different route to avoid the city centre, where the bomb was thrown (this was unplanned). In the confusion, the motorcade continued with the original plan while Franz and Sophie's car moved ahead without the rest of the security personnel. The driver of Franz and Sophie's car took a wrong turn, and another Serbian assassin shot both of them at point-blank range. In retaliation, Austria-Hungary bombed the Serbian capital. Russia, a supporter of Serbia, mobilized against Austria-Hungary. Seeing Russia's intervention, Germany, an ally of Austria-Hungary, attacked Russia and the First World War broke out, which eventually killed 20 million people and wounded 21 million.[1]

> NEVER UNDERESTIMATE THE POWER OF YOUR INTENTION OR A SINGLE ACTION; IT CAN LEAD TO A BUTTERFLY EFFECT.

What Is Chaos Theory?

In the middle of the twentieth century, American mathematician Edward Lorenz, whilst working on

---

[1] 'Franz Ferdinand, archduke of Austria-Este', Britannica, available at https://www.britannica.com/biography/Franz-Ferdinand-Archduke-of-Austria-Este.

weather prediction, propounded **CHAOS theory**, which is 'a mathematical concept that explains that it is possible to get random results from normal equations. The main precept behind this theory is the underlying notion of small occurrences significantly affecting the outcomes of seemingly unrelated events. Chaos theory is also referred to as "non-linear dynamics".'[2]

This means, in the context of life, weather, relationships and complex machine systems, it's difficult to predict the outcome each time since there are a multitude of variables. However, one can see similar patterns in longer cycles, even if the outcome is random each time.

Lorenz also coined the term '**butterfly effect**', which 'rests on the notion that the world is deeply interconnected, such that one small occurrence can influence a much larger complex system'.[3]

In the story narrated above, a wrong turn by a driver led to the First World War, which killed 20 million people, and in theory, one butterfly flapping its wings in Hong Kong can lead to a tornado in Brazil.

If one thinks deeper on the subject, this is true of life. The biggest fights, the biggest arguments and finally, the biggest consequences, stem from the most trivial issues.

The butterfly affect can be felt at the workplace too. Often, the work that employees do, or a single team member does, goes unnoticed in the day-to-day hullabaloo of the workplace. However, sometimes the same unnoticeable work leads to impactful outcomes for the organization and its employees. For example, when an employee performs exceptionally well, their performance results in a positive

---

[2] Clay Halton, 'Chaos Theory: What it is, History, Example', 30 July 2023, available at https://www.investopedia.com/terms/c/chaostheory.asp.

[3] 'Butterfly Effect', Decision Lab, available at https://thedecisionlab.com/reference-guide/economics/the-butterfly-effect.

atmosphere at the workplace. This employee, by their exceptional performance, motivates the employees around them to perform well, which, in turn, encourages other employees to up their performance, eventually benefitting all employees and the company as a whole.

Here comes the second aspect.

Communication

For a leader, communication is key. Regular communication of the team's relevance creates a sense of pride and achievement among team members.

The person working in the corporate environment starts looking out for a new opportunity or a job on account of a lack of effective communication. There is always a trigger that causes a person to start exploring for other opportunities. Once a new job is found, there is over-communication from all corners in the current company, including mentors, superiors, bosses, super-bosses and human resources. But by then, it's too late.

Communication of the relevance of employees' work is important for getting the best out of the employees and for them willingly giving their best.

Communication does not require lengthy monologues from the leader, but dialogue, and more often, just listening, even when no solutions or immediate answers are in sight. Even just a receptive ear can work magic.

What is communication in the real sense?

Communication is simply a transfer of energy. Since human evolution, words have been perceived to have great power. Words are made of letters and letters are made of sounds and sounds are units of energy that are released while having conversations and discussions. It is the simplest and oldest way of transmitting energy. Words create emotions, emotions arouse feelings, feelings create an environment and a sustained environment creates culture.

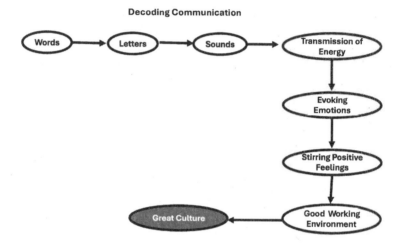

Decoding Communication

Words → Letters → Sounds → Transmission of Energy → Evoking Emotions → Stirring Positive Feelings → Good Working Environment → Great Culture

Communication can be divided into two parts:

a. Prescriptive

b. One that brings perspective

Prescriptive communication involves instructing people what they must do. It is about offering people a fixed formula or rule according to which they should work to solve a problem. This approach has no room for suggestions and deliberations. Prescriptive communication can be damaging as one is not involved in the purpose behind executing a particular task or solving a particular problem. One has no understanding of the reason and the rationale behind the task, and completely misses the bigger picture. *Thus prescriptive communication is transactional and thus yields poor to negative results, even though execution might be swift.*

- The communication that brings perspective ensures that the employee is involved in the visualization of the larger goal that will be achieved now or over time, along with that of the small part being played by the individual or a group of individuals, and thus helping and enabling greater camaraderie and efficiency within the team.

> EVERYONE CHASES AND CLAIMS TO EMPLOY LOGIC, YET THEY ACT AND REACT EMOTIONALLY.

Role of an Employee

From an employee's perspective, what are they providing? Not skills, not talent, not execution, but their precious time? The skills, the work, the talent and the execution can be honed, nurtured and performed. Essentially, in return for a salary, the employee is selling their precious time.

When the employee focuses on using their time appropriately, results come automatically.

State of Seamless Flow

Focus has an interesting aspect known as concentration—the art of putting all one's attention on a single task, getting involved so deeply that the execution happens effortlessly and gets completed before one realizes it. This is also called a state of seamless flow.

The Power and Joy of Concentration

Most musicians and artists, those who relish their craft, get into this state of flow, where they and the universe become one and it feels like the universe is getting everything done exactly as one would wish it. This is the power of concentration.

There are times, after delivering a presentation, when one is just happy with the way the presentation went, without getting worried about the outcome—that is concentration.

Concentration is what one craves. The quality of life is determined by the way one is concentrating on the present task and how one can execute it. Thus, organizations that can define and develop employees who can concentrate reap two benefits.

✓ Satisfaction, joy, happiness and greater expertise in the employee.
✓ Superior results, enabling the growth of the organization.

Shifting gears and making employees as the focal point here.

What can be one edge that can solve for all employees?

And that is helping peers and colleagues in their tasks.

You might ask, why should you undertake someone else's job? But look at it from another viewpoint.

If you help someone else in a task that even you are not prepared or ready for, it pushes, forces, nudges you to learn—to comprehend a new task, to acquire new skills, to become good at something that is not part of you daily routine. As you learn to deliver someone else's results and go beyond simply doing your own job, you learn, widen your horizons and become increasingly relevant in the company, even nearly indispensable.

Why are employees not able to break the glass ceiling and instead, feel stuck, like furniture, in their jobs?

When one is unable to connect the work one does and its relevance in the overall scheme of things, one starts believing that one is stuck in mundane day-to-day activities. Furthermore, doing one's job and not assisting others limits the expanse and horizon of understanding and thus, a feeling of being stuck seeps in.

Another conundrum that one witnesses is popularly known as the **Perception versus Reality Gap.**

'I believe I am handsome, but the world thinks otherwise.' 'The world thinks I am too pushy, while I think I am assertive.'

Perception plays an important role in determining one's future as most decisions about promotions, salary hikes or bonuses, allocating new assignments, understanding strengths and providing new opportunities are made in one's absence by people who have a preformed perception of the person in consideration.

Another problem that perplexes people or corporate workers is:

What should come first—

- ✓ Promotion or
- ✓ Skills, know-how or the vision to handle the new position?

Most desire for the former and ignore the latter.

If one gets promoted to the next level without the skill, foresight and calibre to perform those tasks, then failure, decline and setbacks are certain.

Shouldn't one first learn the tricks, rules and scheme of the next role and start executing it successfully, rather than learning these later?

If one acquires these skills, tricks, vision, foresight and circumspection in advance, and learns to meet the new expectations, it will become imperative for the employer to promote the employee rather than handing the promotion as an aid or a grant in a begging bowl.

If one understands this simple equation, then for such men and women, the glass ceiling doesn't exist.

How can one evaluate one's performance in a corporation when one knows that superiors, bosses and managers work have vested interests and evaluation is always prejudiced?

Input or Output

In many organizations, responsibility and accountability rise without the requisite authority. This leads to helplessness, then frustration and then selfishness in the seniors and thus appraisal, evaluation and final assessment happen on the basis of one's fondness for others rather than objectivity.

Additionally, the system of evaluation focuses only on output and jumps in output without figuring out the input, the process involved in delivering the output and the consistency of the output.

During appraisal cycles, one does not consider that even if the output is not consistent on account of market cycles, disruptions or unforeseen events or situations, a robust process of input and monitoring such input always yields handsome results.

In such a case, how can and how should one evaluate, assess and determine whether one is progressing or regressing?

More often, the salary hike or the bonus one receives based on one's performance is the parameter for one's assessment.

Unfortunately, when inflation is low, firms give low pay hikes or salary increments and when inflation is high, the hikes are relatively higher.

When inflation is high, the company can implement greater price hikes on goods and services, keeping the volumes the same, and so the revenues jump. The opposite happens in a deflationary cycle.

In other words, the macro environment, popular perception and hearsay are judging one's performance rather than one's efforts, endeavours and sustained attempts.

Furthermore, can somebody's judgement of you, your efforts and your results be your real assessment of yourself, your potential and your future?

Not really!

So what's the solution?

What's the answer, what's the formula? What's the methodology?

Measuring one's growth and progress in a corporate environment can be captured by

CFO-1 >CFO-0

Here the CFO stands for free earnings from <u>SKIN</u>.

What does <u>SKIN</u> stand for? In order, it stands for the following four:

✓ **Skill**

Has there been a new skill added during the year?

Has it yielded anything towards one's monetary growth?

Has the new skill benefitted any stakeholder in a meaningful manner?

New skills can be improved articulation, better man management expertise, deeper client relationships through better engagement or perhaps a new role or responsibility that came along and automatically added new skills in the process of executing it.

✓ **Knowledge**

Knowledge is more often confused with information. Knowledge is information, understanding the impact of information, digging deeper to the second- and third-level impact of information, using such information in conjunction with past expertise and experience and applying it in the present context to arrive at desired results through effective decision-making.

As one experiences more outcomes, learns more perspectives, builds more scenarios and uses them for effective decision-making, knowledge is enhanced.

In a business context, employees who use this knowledge to protect and propel the business get rewarded handsomely. These employees can find opportunity in catastrophe and calamity.

The question one needs to ask is whether any enhanced income attained is attributable to such knowledge acquired, amassed or accumulated through the year.

✓ **Improved version or self**

Has one gained maturity, wisdom and clarity in one's life and has one worked on oneself?

Did it benefit oneself in gaining respect, in having more chances, more opportunities and more occasions to solve sticky issues? And has that yielded monetary gains?

✓ **New perspective**

Usually, people go through life with their minds boxed up in the same belief system throughout the years. Sometimes, incidents, events and shake-ups reveal a new dimension of life.

A few purposefully keep exploring these new dimensions and perspectives, and those who do it on an ongoing basis have a better probability of happiness and earnings, both, at the same time. Therefore, every event in your life is important as it has the potential to offer you a new perspective to look at life. It is a good idea to revisit your achievements, failures and moments of happiness as well as sadness at the end of every year and write them down on a piece of paper. This exercise of self-introspection will provide you with an opportunity to better understand yourself. It will enable you to explore your emotions, behaviors and thoughts. By reflecting on your experiences, you will surely gain invaluable insights into what makes you happy, what drives you, and what causes you distress. In a world characterized by distractions, self-introspection helps you discover your purpose in life. It is a useful technique for achieving wellbeing and personal growth.

This enhanced self-awareness also forms the bedrock of course correction, leveraging one's strengths and revealing areas of improvement.

How can one deal with the politics and insecurities in the corporate world?

The answer comes from the Shreemad Bhagwad Geeta, verse 38, chapter 2.

सुखदुःखे समे कृत्वा लाभालाभौ जयाजयौ।

ततो युद्धाय युज्यस्व नैवं पापमवाप्स्यसि !

This means 'fight for the sake of duty, treating happiness and distress, loss and gain, victory and defeat alike. Fulfilling your responsibility in this way, you will never incur sin.'

This way, one stays away from politics and insecurities at the same time.

Targeting the top—Are you ready for it? What do you think and what do the promoters and management think?

Most perform well in a planned environment, but what happens when unplanned, calamitous events strike? How does one react?

What does one prioritize?

What's the mental state when you face tough conditions unexpectedly? The answers to these questions lie in how effectively a person manages their emotions and connect with others.

Dissolving the Disconnect!

> PEOPLE QUIT NOT BECAUSE OF MONEY, WORK PRESSURE OR RESULTS, BUT BECAUSE OF THE ENVIRONMENT.

Emotional acumen is the key aspect that differentiates the CXOs moving up to the next level, leading bigger organizations, from the performers who are left behind.

Emotional Acumen (EA) encompasses two aspects:

✓ Managing one's own emotions
✓ Managing the emotions of others

By developing a strong emotional acumen and with an eye on the end goal, one can achieve not only professional success but also personal success.

Relationships are the key to achieving success in any field. EA focuses on solving the challenges of relationships, whether with a partner, an employee, a vendor, a government official or a shareholder, all of whom have different needs, requirements and perspectives on the same thing.

EA also helps one distinguish between morality, ethics, values and the zeal, emotion and passion to achieve goals.

EA separates emotions from decision-making, though it takes into account the motivation behind the emotions.

EA is critical if one needs to be a good leader, to get tasks accomplished and results delivered with a high level of motivation within the team and the organization.

However, is it always easy to manage emotions? Perhaps not. Remind yourself that every reaction to a situation is transitory and that ultimately, good actions will lead to good outcomes. Therefore, stay calm and cut viciousness out of your thoughts, words and actions.

Let's come back to Priya, who moved ahead and was ready to conquer the corporate world with her kind and helpful approach. She learnt English and became fluent in it, thereby understanding and solving clients' problems in the call centre.

Soon, Priya was promoted to team leader, and eventually to vice president. Her hard work finally yielded results, and she was able to buy a small apartment from her savings, where she brought her siblings and mother to live.

> WHAT WORKS FOR YOU IN ONE ORGANIZATION MAY NOT WORK FOR YOU IN ANOTHER. THIS DOES NOT MAKE YOU A BAD OR WORSE EMPLOYEE.

Learning 1: Comfort, cosiness and cushioning create complacency. Pushing oneself internally, facing failures, wrestling with hardships and adversity causes growth.

Learning 2: One has to be ready for the job, for the opportunity, for the next move by constantly preparing for it and delivering as if one is already in that position. Groundwork and preparation can't be done when one is in the war. When one is at war, one has to fight and not just spend time getting ready for it.

6

Entrepreneurial Enigma—
What's Behind the Scenes?

The Avid, Ardent, Ambitious Priya

Finally, years of toil, effort and exertion bore fruit and Priya changed her family's circumstances. For a change, she was able to eat the wholesome food her mother made for her rather than greasy restaurant food. As her roles changed, the demands, responsibilities, accountability and challenges multiplied.

Now Priya had to maintain a balance between her superiors' expectations of the team's performances and the dynamic business environment represented by the demanding clientele on the calls. The superiors' demands grew incessantly and so did Priya's efforts, as well as time spent in the office between meetings and presentations.

Time Flies, Expectations Multiply

Time flew fast, as though it had wings. The young Priya is now middle-aged, in her mid-thirties and approaching her forties with some strands of white peeking out from among her thick black hair. She had saved, built up a corpus and moved into a big apartment in a good locality on a mortgage. The work was interesting, expansive and never-ending. Weeks turned into months, months into quarters and quarters into years.

Priya had had a ritual for years—she would stop at the next-door bakery and buy a fruit cake for her family every day. The family shared and enjoyed the small fruit cake every day. Sometimes, when Priya was back late, the family missed that mini-celebration that had become a daily practice, a toast to life and another happy day.

As time passed, the cost of the fruit cake jumped. Priya cribbed each time, yet she bought the same cake and didn't stop the practice.

As years went by, the next-door bakery turned into a fast-food eatery serving hot meals, fast food and whatnot. The shop grew into a restaurant-cum-takeaway joint for bakery items.

One evening, after a long day, drained and fatigued, Priya stopped yet again at the bakery. Seeing Priya, the older gentleman at the counter promptly packed the fruit cake and Priya removed a 100 rupee note from her purse. The man said, 'Rs 40 more.' Baffled, Priya said, 'Rs 40? You need to give me Rs 20 back. Isn't the cake for Rs 80? Yesterday, I paid you Rs 80 for the same cake.'

The man said that the prices had gone up, things had become more expensive and the staff's salaries had gone up too.

Priya stared at the man, taking out a fifty-rupee note from her purse and handed it over. The man kindly returned the change to her.

Out of nowhere, Priya asked, 'Uncle, I have been seeing you here for over twelve years and you once mentioned that you have been here for over thirty years. How did you make money over the years?'

The old man was well-acquainted with Priya and knew that she was an ambitious woman with big dreams; she had become more of a friend than a customer. Answering Priya's question, the man replied, 'This shop enabled my two daughters to complete their studies. One is a neurosurgeon now and working in Ahmedabad, and the other is a professor in Bhopal. This shop got my daughters married and took care of my every need. It helped me buy a big 1500 sq. foot house in this city where, after slogging even for decades, people can't afford a slum.' There was a big smile on his face and a glow on his cheeks.

He further said, 'If someone borrows your skills, your talent and your passion to fulfil their ambition, their desires, their aspirations, then your dreams will always remain unfulfilled. After all, you have one life and one try is a must.'

He went on, 'Thirty years back, when I came, I knew nothing. I knew only hard work and the fact that sincere, hard work and quality food never fails. It did magic for me as well. I believe it can do that for anyone.

'I rented this shop from the owner, a Parsi gentleman, and promised that I would give the complete rent after six months as I had no cash with me. I had a gold ring, which served as a deposit, and told him that I would come back and take it from him after six months. I then started to bake buns, put butter and jam in them and began selling them.

'Today I have this shop which I have converted to a small restaurant, a house, savings and all that I need to live a good life.'

Priya took the change and left the place with uncle's words of wisdom echoing in her mind.

The next day, Priya woke up with a gleam in her eyes and the whole day, she kept thinking of the man's words about chasing dreams rather than working for someone else.

Over the weekend, she made a basic business plan, including expenses for the household and for running the business.

Thanks to her learnings from Gautam, she had saved appropriately, spent reluctantly and invested wisely.

She discussed the plan with her mother. Her mother was aghast—things seemed to be settled after a long time, and it felt like havoc was about to strike again.

After a few attempts to persuade the daughter, the mother realized that Priya had made up her mind and that maybe it was the right thing to do.

She gave all her blessings to Priya but told her to start preparing for it in advance, in parallel with her job.

On the auspicious day of Akshaya Tritiya, Priya took Lord Ganesha's blessings and paid the token rent for a small place to set up a restaurant that specialized in making healthy, tasty dosas.

Her mother provided the secret recipe, trained two cooks in dosa preparation and the venture started.

Priya resigned from her job after fifteen long years and got a standing ovation from the top management and her team members, along with an open offer to join back whenever she desired.

Talent, good attitude and good thought are always precious and are always cherished.

The venture took off under the brand 'Moodbidri Masala Dosa'. Within weeks of the launch, the dosas became a hit in the neighbourhood.

Challenges of attrition, cash flows and wastage cropped up, but Priya and her lean team sailed through, breaking even operationally in 1000 days.

Priya realized that the money she was making in the venture was less than what she was making in her previous job where she would get bonuses and incentives beyond her salary. However, long working hours were taking a toll on her health. She was not as young as she had once been.

Unlike the monetary part, Moodbidri Masala Dosa (the name her mother had suggested as she had grown up in that small hamlet, now a prosperous city) was doing well and was recognized across the city.

She decided to expand the venture through the franchise model and monetize the business.

Many took franchises of Moodbidri Masala Dosa, but none of them worked with the passion, devotion and quality with which Priya served her customers. Franchises could neither emulate Priya's warmth and hospitality nor the quality of the cuisine.

The franchise model turned out to be a massive failure, hitting Priya and her business hard. It tainted her brand as well. She soon pulled out, got the franchises to shut down and returned their money.

Two Legs of a Consumer-Centric Brand

Her preservation of the brand and her mother's trust in her—the woman who had always taught her '**trust and quality should never be compromised**'—remained the bedrock of her business.

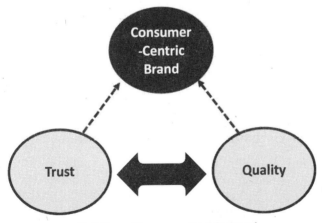

Building a Consumer-Centric Brand

She continued with her outlet but also opened a cloud kitchen. The initial response was great, but Cloud Kitchen Moodbidri Masala Dosa also eventually flopped. By the time the Moodbidri Masala Dosa reached the customer, it was soft and soggy and had lost its taste and appeal.

Setback after setback, no light in sight and the bare minimum money left to continue running the lone outlet—Priya was worried about the future of Moodbidri Masala Dosa, about her own future and her family's future.

She had taken a loan for the house and the EMIs needed to be paid. As of now, she was managing somehow, but her payments to the suppliers were taking longer and longer to scrape together. The suppliers of vegetables, rice and other items were patient, however, as they knew Priya's character.

The Ugly, Unpleasant, Ungainly Side of Entrepreneurship

The pressure was building and so was the doubt—did she do the right thing by quitting her job and starting the venture when everything was nearly perfect in her life?

Dreams need patience. Dreams ask one to pay the price to achieve them and turn them into reality.

The price may not be monetary or physical exertion or hardships. Sometimes, the price is self-doubt, sometimes fear, sometimes dark failure.

Expectations Vs Reality

Expectatation: Reality:

Expectation – One Blip

Reality – Blips Enable Breakthrough

Since life is short, most people want to make most of it. They want to try and fulfil all their dreams, so that they do not have any regrets later. To achieve their dreams, they are willing to push themselves to extremes

> RISK AND INDEPENDENCE, BOTH, ARE A BANE AND A BOON IN BUSINESS.

and take risks including financial ones. Dreams, however, are sometimes too big for our savings and investments. Therefore, take calculated risks and don't put all your money at stake. You may fail, but even if you do, you will have enough left to try again. This failure will teach you a hundred other ways to succeed.

What's your reason?

Many start their own ventures, but the reasons are sometimes inappropriate.

Some start the venture as they are not able to cope with politics in the office, some can't stand the culture of the corporate world, some feel burnt out, some feel that they have hit the glass ceiling and some believe that they can't enhance and upgrade their skills. Some complain of abusive seniors, some complain of favouritism and many believe there is a lack of challenge in their jobs. For some, success on the job is elusive, some face harassment in their jobs and some just don't like their jobs.

Whatever the reason, in the present day, working for a salary and having your own business or start-up is broadly the same. Both require entrepreneurial instincts, both need ownership of the outcome and both place equal emphasis on execution, managing one's own emotions and managing the emotions of others.

Comparison with others leads to disgruntlement and thus comes a time when one decides to start something of one's own.

People generally remain silent and never articulate the real reason why they are starting a new venture.

Often, the feeling inside and the feeling expressed to near and dear ones is one of these two:

a. One is not enjoying the work.

b. One is not able to reach or work to one's peak potential or one is not being utilized to one's optimum capability.

   The conundrum in life is that one never can enjoy every act, every task or every work allocated to one. Enjoyment comes from the people around us and the way work is done. If one collaborates and engages with several cheerful souls with the intent of benefitting others while also earning, then surely, the task becomes enjoyable.

   ✓ An open environment where the focus is on process and outcome, rather than appeasement, words and protocols, always yields creativity and new ideas.

   ✓ On the other hand, most employees don't reach their peak potential because they are selfish and greedy towards their teams, community and peers.

   What if a person, after finishing his or her work, goes and extends one's help to one's peer or someone in another department?

   Wouldn't it help the other person, who is unduly burdened, and make you the first person who learns the skill set of another department as well making you more useful and more relevant for the organization as a whole?

This begs the question of why people become entrepreneurs. To answer this question, it is important to understand the forces that drive us. Behind our every action there are certain motivating factors. Therefore, to anlayse a decision it is critical to understand the forces underlying it. So, why do people choose entrepreneurship?

> IF YOU WISH TO REACH YOUR PEAK POTENTIAL, YOU HAVE TO START YOUR OWN BUSINESS.

1. *Is it sighting a mammoth opportunity that can be capitalized on?*
2. *Or is it to give a try, one try, at least?*
3. *Is it a gigantic problem that needs to be solved that is being experienced by millions of people?*

The answer could be one of the three, two of the three or all the three above.

Whatever the answer may be, one thing is certain—if the problem impacts millions, millions of dollars can be raised to solve the problem, but if the problem is affecting billions, billions will flow in as funds to propel the business.

Why do 1 in 1000 and not 100 see the light at the end of the tunnel?

An entrepreneurial journey starts with an entrepreneurial mindset.

Often, one jumps into a business venture or starts an enterprise without being prepared and without figuring out the mental, emotional and attitudinal challenges one may have to make.

An entrepreneur has:

- No luxury of time

- No luxury to select the type of work they are willing to do

In other words, the entrepreneur can't survive with inhibitions.

Work Pressure

Additionally, if the work pressure in a job looks bad, then as an entrepreneur it is worse. One is constantly feeling the pressure of managing one's family finances, taking care of the running finances of the firm as well as ensuring payments to employees and vendors on time.

Bad Days or Better Days

There are good days and bad days in everyone's life. However, the entrepreneur cannot afford to have bad days. Even if one has such a day, one has to change their mood and get on with the work.

An entrepreneur has to be highly motivated and that motivation should stem from within and not from others, as others will always try to pull them down to get a better deal.

The entrepreneur not only needs to pull themselves up but also keep the team super motivated and excited about even the junk job one is involved in.

The external environment is unpredictable and will always pose challenges that will defy the most detailed planning and all prepared back-ups and resources that can be appropriated in a time of need.

Assumptions fail, the environment suddenly becomes hostile, demand collapses, new technology disrupts, new competition with deep pockets emerges—anything and everything can derail the business.

Thus a can-do, will-do and will-happen attitude is a must, but most lose that confidence within the first 270 days of starting the venture, when they need it most.

Bharat is blessed as it sees high demand for goods and services most of the time. However, it has been found, through several studies foregrounded in ancient wisdom, that the toughest period for any business, venture or start-up is between the 360th day and the 548th day. If businesses can survive through this period, they usually see operating profitability (break-even at an operating or marginal cost level, undermining the fixed costs) between the 1100th day and the 1190th day. Most businesses break even at a profit after tax (PAT) level with fully loaded expenses in 1825 days.[1]

Getting through these 1200 days can be daunting. Three strategies help you get through them and succeed as an entrepreneur.

Surviving Shit

Three hacks that enable the entrepreneurial mindset—the three Bs.

1. **Beer Bottle Bliss:**
   Everyone experiences or has memories of wins, glee, gaiety, accomplishments, achievements and advancements in their lives. Some may have many, some may have few, some have it for long periods and some may have short ones.

---

[1] Ray Zinn, '6 Steps to Surviving 3 Years', Entrepreneur, 3 August 2017, available at https://www.entrepreneur.com/starting-a-business/6-steps-to-surviving-3-years/293522; '60% of New Businesses Fail in the First 3 Years. Here's Why', Durhan City Incubator, 7 November 2019, available at https://dcincubator.co.uk/blog/60-of-new-businesses-fail-in-the-first-3-years-heres-why/.

When your venture is in the doldrums, think of those peaks one has conquered and remember how you felt at the time of accomplishing those feats. Just the memory will help you bounce back, come back on track, push the limits and go on.

Most start-ups fold up for want of money. Maybe the founders have not explored enough funding avenues. Maybe they have gotten tired of narrating their story, potential and vision. Maybe they are lacking just that one pitch that was not made. This phenomenon of resurrecting and remembering one's past triumphs and the bliss one attained and experienced is called **Beer Bottle Bliss**—the same fun, joy and delight one gets after gulping down a beer.

2. **Be in the game to win the game:**

> WHEN YOU FAIL AS AN ENTREPRENEUR, NOT ONLY DO YOU GAIN EXPERIENCE BUT ALSO COURAGE.

One thing is certain—no sustained success can be accomplished without failure. Every entrepreneur faces challenges, collapse and catastrophe at different points in the venture. During those testing times, one needs to just survive and sail through those hard periods.

When one can't see the light at the end of the tunnel, just keep moving one step at a time, focus on the next step, next action, next hour, next day and next week. Forget about the month, quarter or year. Just keep moving forward with baby steps. Simply put, **take one step at a time.**

One has to be in the game to win the game. The ones who perish can never win the game.

3. **Baking the Bigger Picture:**
   Failure, rejection and defeat lead to self-doubt, anger and frustration, and that triggers a negative spiral.

   Why did one start, what was the idea and what was the thought, the vision? Remembering these things energizes oneself when one is surrounded by hopelessness.

   Painting or building the bigger picture brings encouragement, motivation and drive that leads to small actions, which leads to consistent progress, which builds momentum, and momentum inspires bigger actions, leading to bigger outcomes.

Born an Entrepreneur! Everyone is an Entrepreneur!

Sometimes, the best idea, the highest capability and the cleanest solution remain in the mind and turn into regrets, only because of fear.

✓ Humans are born to be entrepreneurs. Every professional is an entrepreneur, every worker is an entrepreneur as they are managing their time to maximize output, and every creative person or artist is an entrepreneur as they want acknowledgement and appreciation of their performance or work.

✓ When a child is convincing their parents to buy them a certain product, the entrepreneur in them is at work, convincing others why this product is essential for their well-being. It's just the reverse when the child grows up and convinces others to buy the product that has been created, now by that entrepreneur.

✓ When the parents are running the household with limited resources and optimizing them to fulfil the needs of the family, it brings out the natural instincts of an entrepreneur, who always has to struggle with limited capital and deploy that limited capital in a manner that yields the highest possible growth for the business.

✓ When a youth plays a team sport, managing the temperaments of the other players and keeping them focused on the larger goals while focusing on individual performances and individual aspirations, is a classic example of how team management and optimum use of limited human resources is done when one starts a business.

PIVOT, AND KEEP MOVING.

The ability to come up with an idea, to execute it and to pursue victory with a passion is present in all humans, but fear stops one from pursuing the dreams of their choice. Failure, complacency and shame all emanate out of fear and that is the single biggest reason why, despite having skills, ideas and passion, people continue in corporate slavery.

Since the dawn of human history, all the systems that have been created and those which exist today are an outcome of **entrepreneurial spirit.**

The barter system, trade and technology, three landmarks in human history, all represent entrepreneurial spirit.

Humans are not content to follow orders, to be bossed around, and are not fine with being rebuked by their superiors when they are in a foul mood. They love their freedom, their independence, their ability to create something new.

Why do many think, a few start and a handful of selected ones succeed?

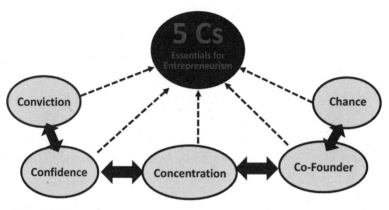

5 Cs Philosophy

I. **Conviction:**

When a person starts a venture believing in what they have started and why they have started it, when they help users, customers and the world in solving some challenges, past and present, that is conviction.

Believing that the solution developed works and will continue to work, and making others believe it too, is the first step.

II. **Confidence:**

The next step is to pitch the same thing again and again, thousands of times, to every vendor from whom one needs credit, to the potential buyer who intends to buy the product, whether a good or a service, to the financier or the venture capitalist or the angel investor who will write the initial cheque, without even knowing whether the start-up will survive the first couple of years or not.

> WHEN EVERYONE HAS LEFT YOU ALONE, GO BACK TO THE COMPANY OF YOUR THOUGHTS— WHY AND WHEN YOU STARTED.

Confidence in the product and usage case attracts money, perhaps more than what the pedigree of the founders would.

Many naysayers will block the path and shake the confidence with multiple rejections, but the founder has to get up and look at the hope of yet another bright day, having another chance, another opportunity to get a yes.

One needs to constantly be engaged in self-talk:

'I have it in me.'

'I can do it.'

'I will do it; it will get done.'

III. **Concentration:**

Distractions are galore, but concentrating on the venture is key. Sleeping, breathing, and living the venture and finally executing it effortlessly lead to the first step on the achievement staircase.

For the first few years after a child comes into the family, they are the centre of attraction as well as the primary focus. Attention and care both are needed for the child to get through the initial years and so is the case with the venture. As mentioned earlier, when ventures cross the critical and painful first 1,100 days, the probability of their survival multiplies manifold.

IV. **Complementary co-founder:**

A start-up entails round-the-clock work and most individual founders believe that it can be done by one person. But when the chips are low, when times are tough and when no one understands the situation, the co-founder, the buddy, the sounding board listens and enables.

Furthermore, most humans have a liking for either public-facing roles or solitary ones. Those who are good with sales, marketing and business development might lack interest in and the skill sets for running operations and servicing. Those who are good with tech, deep tech, don't wish to go door to door to explain the product or deal with multiple vendors and haggle.

Complementary skill sets in the form of complementary co-founders can work magic.

For many, a start-up is a hobby, for some it's a backup, for others, it's just to gain experience of how it feels, and none of it works as nothing beats passion, motivation and dedication. No amount of money can replace these innate qualities essential for succeeding in a start-up.

The concept of the Silent Hand: The co-founder also works at a subconscious level as a silent hand, as somebody who is watching one's back. It may or may not end up being used very often, but the presence of that silent hand gives psychological support. If a co-founder is not that silent hand, an entrepreneur will seek that in a family member, friend or mentor who will come to the rescue psychologically and emotionally.

V. **Chance:**
Entrepreneurs use gut, intuition and probability and place bets. They always have less than the required money and less than available bandwidth to cope with things, and thus, start-ups need to prioritize a market, a product, a service or the kind of customers they need to go after.

Often, there is no data available for the new product or its usage. The more one explores, the deeper one digs into the market, the more one gauges the habits, behaviour and mannerisms of the market, the more information one gathers, and on the basis of that data, some intuition and some market checks, money is invested to develop demand in that particular market, which may or may not work. *Thus, chance, unparalleled risks and educated guesstimates can lead to unparalleled wins in the form of unparalleled outcomes.*

What Not to do as an Entrepreneur?

Attend to everything:

As an entrepreneur, one is accountable for everything, from the licences to compliance, from the finance to the customer service. However, attending to everything all the time means no time for future growth, future strategy and further execution.

In life, there are only two things that are limited—human bandwidth and capital. Unfortunately, both are extremely scarce, especially for an entrepreneur.

The least focus is on things that are not urgent, yet are important from a sustenance, survival and growth viewpoint.

As an entrepreneur, one has to forge relationships of trust and entrust several urgent tasks to ensure day-to-day execution remains seamless and one eye remains on future growth.

To burn or to build bridges?

During the entrepreneurial journey, one meets several people and every time one meets someone new, one believes that person can be of help in one way or the other. However, nearly 95 per cent of people reject the opportunity,

4.9 per cent keep dithering and only 0.1 per cent show interest in proceeding with the next round of discussions and conversations. These 99.9 per cent of people are not rejections, but potential patrons, collaborators, clients, suppliers or financiers.

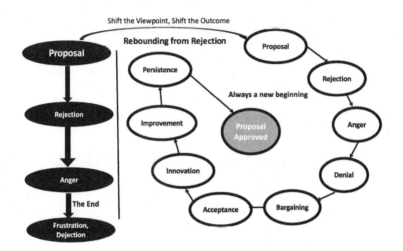

Health in Wealth

An entrepreneur can never compromise on their health—time loss, focus loss or concentration loss due to ill health can be extremely expensive and can cost the entrepreneur dearly.

Even an hour of investment in health daily can lead to a significant jump in the prospects of the start-up as it brings fresh ideas, positive thinking as well new zeal for execution.

Sometimes, working too hard, overthinking, burdening the mind with worries about future growth lead to stress and exhaustion. Is it true?

Does one gain something from getting stressed?

Why do people say stress is bad?

Perhaps stress increases **productivity**, stress increases one's **ability** to deal with situations.

Let's evaluate.

For some, stress **clouds clear thinking** and forces one to act irrationally and irresponsibly. And one is well aware of the fact that every action has consequences. Can these consequences arising out of clouded thinking arising out of stress be measured?

#ROST or **Return on Stress Taken**

But before understanding the concept of #ROST let's refresh the concept of #ROTI or Return on Time Invested.

#ROTI = Savings generated by spending extra time on the same activity. For example, if one has bought a product from Amazon for Rs 500 after spending 10 minutes on Coupon Dunia to save 20 per cent, one has saved Rs 100 in 10 minutes. Thus, ROTI is 100*60/10 = Rs 600 per hour.

#ROST = It is directly linked to the ROTI. **Return on Stress Taken** is incremental earnings generated due to heightened stress followed by earnings lost due to downtime for recovery. For example, let's say a person drives for Uber and is paid Rs 250 for every ride. After every five rides, he moves to the next bracket, where he earns 10 per cent (without compounding) more than the previous slab right from the first ride. He has an average of eleven rides in 24 hours. But one day, he pushes himself to complete twenty-one rides in a 24-hour span and earns Rs 7350 instead of Rs 3300.

Due to the extra stress and effort, however, he slept for 4 more hours the next day and missed half a day of work. He could only complete six rides the next day. Thus, his **#ROST** will be = 7350 − 3300 − 1650 = 2400. If ROST creates more downtime than your routine productivity, then it's negative.

Thus, one of the things entrepreneurs need to watch is meetings and appraisals. **Meetings and appraisals should be used as learning and engagement opportunities, or the ROST of these interactions will always be negative.**

How can entrepreneurship be honed, nurtured and promoted?

Being resilient is a habit, and all good habits can be developed.

Since time immemorial, necessity, need and deprivation have driven human instincts.

The ecology, topography and surroundings create the environment that moulds individual behaviour. Therefore, if the environment is positive, an individual, despite constraints, starts looking for opportunities. Some people make most of these opportunities and become super successful, and they, thus, become role models for others.

Japan

A simple concept to bring greater efficiency to the manufacturing process is **Just–in–time (JIT)**. The concept emerged in Japan after the Second World War and the devastation it caused.

The impact of the Second World War (1939–1945) on Japan was so grave that it completely shattered its economy. Most of its infrastructure and industrial plants were destroyed. The war cost Japan approximately 2.6 to 3 million lives and 56 billion USD.[2]

---

[2] 'The Japanese Economic Miracle', Berkeley Economic Review, 26 January 2023, available at https://econreview.berkeley.edu/the-japanese-economic-miracle/.

Major parts of Tokyo and many other cities were burnt to ashes. One-third of Japan's wealth was destroyed.

But the Japanese decided to resurrect the country and thus, JIT came into existence, among many other concepts. The JIT methodology, also known as the lean production model, is commonly associated with manufacturers in post-Second World War Japan. Faced with a lack of working capital and natural resources, Japanese companies had to incorporate lean, efficient business practices into their manufacturing processes. This meant building smaller factories and producing items in smaller batches while paying close attention to the efficiency of their production processes.

It endeavoured to eliminate seven types of ills in production: overproduction, waiting, excess inventory, transportation costs, processing delays, motion hindrance and defects.

As Japan started to increase production, the country didn't have enough space, and so the assembling of parts would happen on the ship in a manner that the automobiles would be ready for delivery as soon as the ship hit the shores of the importing country.[3]

North India

Similarly, in India, people residing in the northern states of India are perceived as aggressive, as they have been attacked by invaders, thugs and dacoits for over one and a half

[3] Robert Sheldon, 'just-in-time manufacturing', TechTarget, available at https://www.techtarget.com/whatis/definition/just-in-time-man-ufacturing-JITmanufacturing#:~:text=The%20JIT%20methodolo-gy%2C%20also%20known,practices%20into%20their%20man-ufacturing%20processes; 'Just-in-Time Manufacturing: The Path to Efficiency', Businessmap, available at https://businessmap.io/lean-man-agement/pull/just-in-time-production.

millennia and their temperament has been altered by that over the centuries.

Uttarakhand

Another example of the environment contributing to the cause is young men joining the military. One of the largest contributors to this is the state of Uttarakhand. On account of a hilly topography, the terrain and climate are challenging and landslides and avalanches are frequent occurrences, so hill residents are physically and mentally strong and thus are suited for contributing to Mother India through their prowess in military warfare.

Singapore

One of the surveys conducted by the World Economic Forum in 2019 uncovered something surprising—a very small proportion of Singaporeans, barely 17 per cent, wish to become entrepreneurs, and that they would prefer to be in Singapore than work abroad.[4]

Singapore has a secure, low-crime, rules-oriented culture and so most young people who have been born and bred there find it difficult to move into unchartered territory with unpredictable, dynamic work and environments. Furthermore, entrepreneurship brings challenges, uncertainty and unexpected outcomes and, therefore, Singaporeans

---

[4] Kimberly Lim, 'Few Singaporean youths aim to be entrepreneurs, most have no plans to work overseas: WEF survey', Today Online, 16 August 2019, available at https://www.todayonline.com/singapore/singapore-youths-come-last-survey-six-nations-entrepreneurial-ambition#:~:text=In%20terms%20of%20entrepreneurial%20ambition,of%20youths%20expressing%20this%20aspiration.

have been less likely to start their own ventures than being employed.

On the other hand, the United States, as stated earlier, has a culture of fighting and survival. The US is the hub of immigrants. Immigrants face and fight tough challenges throughout their adult lives, starting with the circumstances that force them to leave their home countries. Thus, one can see that more than 10 per cent of US billionaires, including the founders of Tesla, Nvidia, PayPal, Google, Calendly and Zoom, are immigrants. These entrepreneurs have created value for themselves and for the nation.

Thus, environment, culture and circumstances play a vital role in an entrepreneurial journey.

However, what is critical for becoming an entrepreneur can be summed up in three simple things, all of which can be inculcated through an environment conducive to entrepreneurship.

I. **Deprivation:**
   Some hunger, struggle and privation build endurance and the emotional, physical, mental and psychological ability to survive hardship. One of the many reasons why longer fasts are observed across religions, including Hindutva, Jainism and Islam, is to inculcate grit and determination. Also, less or no food intake keeps the mind alert and one can remember and pray to the Almighty better with no or a little food intake.

II. **Curiosity:**
   A culture in which the family allows and even encourages the questioning of everything, from the system and the process to even the terminology, creates a curious mind. That curiosity, when met with practical life challenges and with limited or no

solutions in sight, leads to business ideation or the birth of new economic opportunities.

III. **Freedom:**

Human life's greatest desire is freedom—the freedom to be who one is, the freedom to express oneself and the freedom to pursue one's passions creates entrepreneurial instincts.

Societies that give individuals freedom and allow them to explore their callings and flourish create successful and happy entrepreneurs.

Formula to Evaluate Entrepreneurial Success at Every Juncture

A start-up needs funds to grow and that is where venture capital comes into the picture. Venture capitalists fund new businesses that have growth potential. These start-ups have no access to the listed equity market and can't raise debts due to insufficient cash flows. Venture capitalists use the money of their investors to fund start-ups. Therefore, in venture capital funding there are three parties involved: the venture capital firm, its investors and the founders or entrepreneurs who receive the funding. The success of every entrepreneurial venture is, therefore, crucial for the success of the parties involved in it. Since venture capital firms are answerable to their investors they keep a close eye on how the companies funded by them perform. They closely track the fundamentals and financials of these companies and even set sales and revenue targets for them. The belief that eventually, the businesses will make money and turn profitable guides their actions.

The world has a single parameter for assessing the success of a start-up—the last round of valuations. However, valuations of the start-up in real terms can't conclusively convey whether the start-up is progressing or not.

Higher valuations can be given to the start-up on account of the idea, on account of the personality of the founder or founders or the connections or networks of the founder.

But at any point, how can one ascertain whether the start-up is growing or not?

Here's an uncomplicated formula:

$$CFO_1 > CFO_0$$

Here, CFO means cash flows from the new market, new product, new stream, new usage, new clients or new territories.

And the question to be asked every quarter is: is the business growing?

Priya's Next Pivot

Despite the pivot she gave it, Priya's second failure in the venture shook her. What next, she wondered.

As always, when Priya was confused, she would take the advice of her mother—her benefactor, her patron and her first teacher.

On the last Saturday of the month, Priya was sitting on a rocking chair, wondering how the salaries would be paid this month as the cloud kitchen sales had dipped and the restaurant had also had fewer visitors due to heavy rains in the last couple of months.

Her mother came to her and started running her hands through Priya's grey hair. Priya started crying profusely. Her mother had not seen such a weak, broken and shaken up Priya in a long time.

Before her mother could ask anything, Priya narrated the entire ordeal. Her mother remained silent and heard the entire saga with great composure, without uttering a word. After a couple of hours, her mother said, 'It's very late, both of us should go off to sleep.'

Priya was sad, drowsy and dejected, but sleep did not come to her. Priya thought, my mother is a simpleton from a village, how would she understand the challenges of a business and a start-up? But in her heart, she was also grateful that her mother's presence was giving her mental support, an anchor in her life when she needed it most.

Just One, Only One

During good times, one has a lot of friends with whom one parties and shares one's good fortune, but when tough times begin, one only needs one person in this entire world, just one on whom one can fall back— maybe a friend, maybe a relative, maybe a spouse, a sibling or a parent. Just one is all one needs, but sometimes, it is just that one that we don't get.

> YOU NEED ONLY ONE PERSON IN THIS WORLD TO WATCH YOUR BACK UNCONDITIONALLY, TO MORALLY AND PHYSICALLY STAND BEHIND YOU, AND YOU WILL CONQUER THE WORLD.

Priya was lucky—she had her mother as the pillar, supporting her in thick and thin.

The Teaching

The next day, her mother got up early, woke Priya up and told her that some of her village relatives were coming for brunch and mother and daughter needed to prepare some tasty dosas for them.

Priya thought how inconsiderate her mother was—here she was, reeling under such severe pressure, and her mother had invited some guests over for lunch.

Nonetheless, she got ready. But Priya was in no mood to cook the dosas and prepare food for over ten guests.

Priya told the mother that pick-up from the cloud kitchen has been limited anyway and the batter would go to waste, so she would get the dosas prepared and delivered to the house for the guests.

Her mother said, 'Great idea, let's call for food for ten people.'

Priya asked how she would know how many dosas the ten guests would eat? And what if they don't eat? The dosas will become soggy. Also, some may want extra masala, some may want extra gunpowder (special masala for Moodbidri Masala Dosa) and some may want more vegetables.

Her mother immediately replied, 'Priya, you are right. Why don't you call for the batter and dry masala separately and we will make dosas as per each guest's preference, serving them hot?'

Priya liked the idea and got the batter, the masala and the other ingredients from the cloud kitchen.

Her mother insisted that Priya should make the dosas while she served the guests. Priya followed her mother's suggestion as she was not in the right frame of mind to serve and have polite conversations with the guests. This way, Priya thought she would avoid any chit-chat about the venture and the business too, which everyone in the family knew had nose-dived after its initial success.

The guests were delighted with the dosas and raved about Priya's proficiency.

In the afternoon, both mother and daughter were clearing the kitchen and Priya's mother told Priya that when she had come to this city, she had nothing. Even if she, Priya, needed to sell her house or her belongings to pay off the dues of her vendors or her employees, she shouldn't be afraid, as her mother believed that Priya could restart.

> SILENTLY OBSERVE YOUR CLIENTS AND THEIR BEHAVIOUR; IT WILL GIVE YOU THE BEST MARKETING INSIGHTS TO MULTIPLY DEMAND.

She continued further motivating Priya by reminding her that when she came here, she had nothing—no experience, knowledge or even the skills to communicate or converse. Today, she has all of it and the best part— she has the experience of knowing what doesn't work. Her mother said, 'Don't be scared, child, everything will be fine and will come back on track.'

Her mother's words gave Priya confidence and courage. Resting on the bed, she suddenly realized that though the batter and masala had been prepared by the chefs, helpers and cooks in the cloud kitchen, she had got all the praise.

The next day, all charged up, Priya, started instructing the team to prepare the batter in a manner that would last for 48 hours at room temperature and 72 hours if refrigerated, and the dry masala so that it would last for seven days at room temperature.

She started piloting this by putting the batter plus masala on sale in her eating joint. Whoever came to eat fresh dosas at the eatery also picked up one batter packet due to the heavy rains.

By now, Priya had learnt the tricks of sales and demand creation. Whoever came to eat at the eatery, the staff ensured that Moodbidri Masala Dosa's call centre hand phone number was saved in their phone and was put on speed dial if the guest agreed. They tied up with a delivery service so that a delivery could be made anywhere in the city within forty-five minutes.

The business picked up, demand was mammoth and Priya's fortunes turned. From meagre sales of Rs 2000 per day, her turnover moved up to Rs 20 lakh per day, with extensive distribution coverage through cold storage vans. Margins were high, the product was simple and logistics were easy.

Further, to keep the product fresh, Priya's mother suggested that unsold and unused batter be cooked every night between 8 and 9 p.m. and be distributed to children from the nearby slums. When other helpers were preparing to soak the pulses and rice for the next day, two cooks quickly prepared the dosas and distributed the food.

The business reached new heights. Priya's zeal and her endeavour to give back to society, both yielded results.

Learning 1: Fail Fast, Fail Cheap—The entrepreneurial journey is never a straight line. When in trouble, pivot as many times as needed, but survive. At its peak, expand the expanse of the business.

Learning 2: Endless Execution—Success and efforts are always disproportionate. Initial efforts lead to a disproportionately lower outcome, but with patience, persistence and perseverance, after the inflection point, small efforts lead to a disproportionately higher quantum of success.

Learning 3: Money Matters—Fundraising is the key to survival. The first two seconds accompanied by the elevator pitch, can either do wonders for the venture or cause irreparable harm.

7

Having Happiness or Maximizing
the Happiness Quotient

Rags to Riches

Priya toiled day and night and left no stone unturned to expand the business. She realized that to create high demand for her products, she would need to establish a large distribution network. Both pull and push demand were needed. Quality, consistency and experience would create pull but PR, marketing, micro-advertising and brand and image building would create push demand.

She appropriately utilized microblogging sites and social media, talking about the origins of Moodbidri Masala Dosa (MMD), and used tasters, influencers and food bloggers to create visibility, yet remained focused on supply chain management. She knew that if the product was unavailable when the customer wanted it, the demand would be lost and so she ensured all retailers had her products stocked when it was needed.

Most of her products were needed between 7 and 10 a.m., especially when the lady of the house was preparing lunch for her children or for her husband. On weekends, demand surged between 10.30 a.m. and 12 noon when unexpected guests or visitors were arriving, or when the lady was feeling a bit lazy about preparing the ingredients or when she was feeling unwell or when the house help had taken the day off and the lady of the house had all the household chores as well as the cooking to do.

She knew that she had to slowly migrate her product, her food brand and her cooking from **want to need.** The migration was slow, but she invested all her time, energy and money into it.

From Delhi to the entire National Capital Region (NCR), from NCR to Uttar Pradesh, Bihar, Rajasthan and the entire northern belt, Priya expanded her product's reach handsomely.

Her brothers, who had been sheltered from difficulties by her and her mother, had grown up. They were not engaged in the business but couldn't find joy and steady employment in other jobs either. Both graduated, but with limited skill and limited fire in the belly. Both kept shifting jobs, cribbing about lack of freedom at some places, lack of challenge at others and lots of back-biting and politics at yet others.

As the business grew, it needed more hands and finally, they were both inducted into the business.

One was sent to Mumbai and one was sent to Chennai to establish the distribution network. After some initial hiccups, challenges and problems, they learnt the tricks of the trade, expanded the business, got married and got busy with work.

From Vertical to Horizontal Expansion of the Brand

Moodbidri Masala Dosa batter and other products captured the shelf space both in neighbourhood *kirana* stores as well as the large-format retail outlets. Priya realized that now the distribution funnel had been created and thus the marginal cost was minimal. Hence, she started using free cash flows to develop other products.

She expanded from masala dosa batter to idli batter, khaman mixture, dhokla preparation, halwa preparation and upma preparation.

Laser-Sharp Focus

Despite expanding to a wide variety of products, her focus on two things remained laser-sharp.

✓ End User of the Product: The Lady of the House

For her business, the lady of the house was the decision-maker. Her products were targeted at making the life of the homemaker and the working woman easier.

All advertisements, marketing, micro-blogging, PR and cognitive marketing were used to drive home the fact that Moodbidri Masala Dosa was an enabler of the lady of the house, helping her achieve her freedom to do the things that she likes to do by freeing up her time preparing things and not replacing her cooking with ready-to-eat food either.

Priya realized that the lady of the house wished to take care of the family, children, husband, parents and parents-in-law first, before making any time for herself. She got a lot of joy when she cooked food for the family with love, affection and interest.

However, in the lower middle class, there is often no house help and thus the lady has to do all the cooking and other household chores by herself. For the middle class and upper middle class, the practice of hiring cooks in urban centres is increasing but, often, that doesn't satisfy the woman as it's seen as replacing her food with another person's. MMD ensured that the relevance of the lady as the centre of the household, through her food, remained unquestioned. Food is the basic necessity for any and every human being and the one who controls the food of the house remains in control.

✓ Experience of the End Product: Serving Hot Food

Priya ensured that all her preparations involved heating something up, whether through an electric stove or cooking gas.

Psychologically, the cooking or preparation isn't finished till fire or heat is used.

Even when ice cream is made at home, the lady of the house heats the milk and makes it thick to give a better ice cream experience to the family.

Thus, the preparation feels incomplete without heat or fire.

Furthermore, piping hot, freshly cooked food brings the family together. At such times, when the food is being enjoyed by the family, the cooking and recipes of the lady of the house are appreciated in a mini-get-together that happens every day at the dining table.

Priya would always say, '**After all, who doesn't like freshly cooked, piping hot meals?**
These two principles were deeply ingrained in every employee at the time of orientation and were re-emphasized through various methods every quarter—events, webinars, talk shows, quizzes and recognition ceremonies.

Soon, Moodbidri Masala Dosa (MMD) became a household name, and mothers used **MMD's** recipes to teach their daughters to cook.

The business flourished, the firm went public, and Priya was on the cover page of leading magazines, with headlines like:

'Transforming Food'

'Transforming Families'

In a world where brands, gadgets and consumerism are breaking away from family values and bonding, **MMD endeavoured** to bring families together with the mother's food being the binding force, enabled by MMD.

Since the focal point of all ads and PR was the woman of the house, even 'woke' critics couldn't derail the campaign.

The campaign was simple: **'Food, Family, Fun'; fun not only for those who are eating but for the one who is cooking too.**

Journey from the Material World to the Cosmic World That Lies Within Oneself

The firm grew, the business grew and the employees grew. Along with it, the home of the mother, now eighty-five years old, and the daughter, now sixty-two years old, also grew bigger and larger.

FOCUSED CAPITAL ALLOCATION AND FOCUSED ATTENTION BOTH HELP MULTIPLY BUSINESS AS WELL AS HAPPINESS.

Priya bought a mansion in Delhi and had everything she had desired when she started her journey to independence.

But interview after interview, cover page after cover page and award after award didn't give her joy.

She had everything she could think of but that didn't give her happiness.

Sometimes, Priya would think, after all, this is what I struggled for throughout the years.

She would only look forward to an hour in the evening every day when the day's leftover batter (due to expire in a few days) would be used to prepare the dosas that would be served to underprivileged children from the slums.

She would sometimes wonder if something was wrong with her.

Substance Abuse

Deep in her thoughts one day, Priya reminisced about the time a few years back when her youngest brother, Hari, had been sent to Chennai to start the business development activity and expand operations and demand in that region.

The boy who never smoked, drank or had any bad habits went berserk. In his first time away from the protected home environment, away from his mother and sister, with money to spare, Hari started meeting boys who were smoking and drinking. Soon, in an attempt to look cool, smart and adventurous, Priya's young sibling tried a drug cocktail at a party. In no time, occasional parties became frequent get-togethers, those subsequently turned into late nights every night, and with drug availability, drug usage became common.

He got into drugs because of a honey trap—young women addicted to drugs themselves were forced to seduce naive, moneyed young men like Priya's brother Hari, encourage them to try drugs and slowly and steadily ensure that they got addicted.

Priya recalled the dark nights when her mother and she would repent sending Hari to Chennai and would think that it was better to be poor than to have a life where one has spoiled children.

She also remembered the conversation with her mother when she had said, '**Children are the greatest source of happiness—continuous, non-stop happiness—but may also be the source of the greatest grief.**' **This was the single biggest reason why, she had said, a few with money and many without money remain unhappy.**

Life Turning Upside Down

Priya was still astonished at how her life had turned topsy-turvy when she had got the news that Hari had hit a girl hard when high, and that the girl was in a coma and her brother was behind bars.

Priya, who had never met a cop in her life and had never seen the lock-up, had to visit jail multiple times to ensure her brother was out.

> AS INDIA PROGRESSES ECONOMICALLY, MONEY WILL COME EASY, BUT WELLNESS AND RELATIONSHIPS WILL DIMINISH. KEEP A TAB ON THEM.

Priya also remembered how she had to beg the parents of the girl to withdraw the case, pay all her hospitalization expenses and a whopping sum of Rs 5 crore after she was discharged from the hospital.

After that, Priya brought Hari to Delhi but there was no change in him. He was still aggressive and was abusive towards everyone in the family.

The Cure, the Remedy, the Healing

Priya's mother then started a ritual—each morning, she would put on the Vishnu Sahastranama (1000 names of Lord Vishnu, the one who takes care of the cosmos and everything in it) at 5 a.m. on a low volume. When Hari would wake up and have his breakfast, his mother would sit with him and narrate stories from the Upanishads.

The food prepared for Hari had a lot of turmeric, cardamom, cinnamon and clove to remove the *tamas* in him and increase his *satvik* energies. In the night, Priya's mother would put on the Lalita Sahastranama (1000 names of Goddess Lalita, an incarnation of Goddess Lakshmi) as Hari hit the bed.

During the day, Priya's mother ensured that soft, healing music was on in the house throughout the day so that Hari's mood remained buoyant.

The first twenty-one days were tough and there was no improvement in his tantrums and behaviour. But from the twenty-second day, things started to improve. Hari started to read, study and listen to music. His misbehaviour, anger and anxiety reduced dramatically.

In ninety days, there was a sea change. In 180 days, he was back in the office, handling meetings and clients.

After a year of discipline, Hari requested to be sent back to Chennai so that he could close that chapter and move on with his life.

Initially, Priya and her mother were sceptical, but Hari insisted and finally, the mother and the daughter agreed.

After reaching Chennai, Priya's brother went straight to the girl's house, apologized profusely for his behaviour and expressed repentance and remorse.

Apart from his business and work, Hari started a school where all the underprivileged girls from the slums and nearby villages were taught and trained to prepare Moodbidri Masala Dosa and its ingredients. Then they were given a food cart with an initial sum as seed money so they could earn a living. Some of them chose not to start their own business but become cooks and chefs in restaurants and hotels instead.

Priya and her mother were most proud when one of these trainees was hired by the Taj Group, one of the most respected hotel chains in the world, and Hari was invited to talk about his journey of MMD Bhojan Vidyalaya.

Some of the students from MMD Bhojan Vidyalaya went to Germany, the UK and Dubai, working in restaurants serving Indian cuisine.

From Hari's perspective, it served two purposes:

- ✓ It changed the lives of many, who otherwise stood no chance to have a respectable life in society.
- ✓ It democratized the brand of Moodbidri Masala Dosa forever.

    Now every restaurant and eatery, not only in India but globally, was serving Moodbidri Masala Dosa.

    Today, when everything was going well, Priya was thinking, **'Why am I still restless?'**

Why are people with money and people without money both unhappy?

Why is happiness transient and not perpetual?

Why, when one desire is satiated, does the next emerge?

The answer is **Ananda!**

What is Ananda? How can one attain it?

There is no word quite like Ananda in the English language.

Happiness is mostly perceived as Ananda but happiness is a temporary *or* momentary state which is attained when one achieves the desired goal, sees something favourable or acquires something which satiates any of the five senses.

Ananda is beyond the senses. Ananda is a state of mind, body and soul and one can remain in such a state in perpetuity, irrespective of the external environment or surroundings.

Happiness in the present world or Kalyug is felt in matters related to *artha* (money) or *kama* (pleasure, desire).

Bliss also is believed to be a close approximation of Ananda but again, it's not Ananda. Though bliss denotes supreme happiness, utter joy or contentment, it's transient and can change quickly with a change in the outside world.

What is Ananda, then?

One of the most comprehensive explanations of 'Ananda' is found in the **Ananda Valli of Taittiriya Upanishad,** which states that Ananda is a feeling of joy, happiness and pleasures giving way to self-knowledge.

A state of **non-duality between object and subject.** A state of **complete surrender or oneness with Brahma** (Almighty, Supreme God, universe), renouncing the fruits of one's actions and submitting oneself completely to the divine will, leading to the final termination of the cyclical process of life and death.

Ananda is a divine concept—when one sees the divine within oneself and in everyone around one, the feeling of Ananda arrives.

When one overcomes one's animal instincts and gives up one's feeling of mental prowess (ego, *ahankara*, self-preservation), Ananda can be attained.

Ananda is made of two words: **ā** and *nanda.*

Nanda means joy, delight and bliss and **ā** means the highest level.

To live a life of Ananda, one should always be focused on *Sat-cit-ananda* or *Sacchidānanda.*

Sat-cit-ananda or Sacchidānanda means:
Sat or Satya—Truth, complete truth
Chit—Soul
Ananda—State of happiness or bliss in perpetuity
In other words, the state of soul is always bliss. These worldly attractions and attachments that are non-permanent create unhappiness.

Ananda takes consciousness to a higher level even above all three *gunas—sattogun, rajas* and *tamas*.

When one gets **connected with the Atma** (Soul) within oneself, or the Jivatma, or when one's consciousness is focused on one's Jivatma, then Ananda is attainted.

When **Jivatma (one's soul)** gets consciousness or a connection with Param-Atma (cosmic consciousness), **Param-Ananda** is achieved.

Anger, conflicts and wars can be avoided if one realizes how small (*sookshma*) one is in the cosmos. This thought itself can bring humility.

The formation of the earth and human life took millions of years and one is only here on this planet for a few years or a century at best—this thought itself can pave the way towards one's journey of achieving Ananda.

Practising Ahinsa not only with fellow human beings but with every creature on the planet will enable one to think about wholesomeness and will take one a step closer to Ananda.

How can one attain Ananda?

1. One should start following the concept of **Brahma Satyam Jagat Mithya**.

'Brahma Satyam, Jagat Mithya, Jeeva Brahmaiva Na Param'

(ब्रह्म सत्यं जगन्मिथ्या जीवब्रह्मैवनापरम).

Advaita Vedanta mentions three entities of **Jeev, Jagat and Ishwara,** which seem different to the naked eye. Underlying these three entities is only one reality, a single unity of the entire universe—the appearance of Brahma.

2. **Brahma Dhyan**—For 5 minutes every day, at a designated time, one should start being a Brahma Chari—focusing on oneness with Brahma (for the first three weeks, it will be a challenge sitting with emptiness, no thought. After that, one will start experiencing joy in that state, and the path to Ananda will emerge).

3. **Gratitude to Brahma**—Being thankful to the divinity for what has been given to oneself.

4. **Evolution**—The feeling that evolution happened through millions/billions of years and one is not responsible for it but is an outcome of it.

   In essence, there is no prescription. One should start with steadfast will and one will learn.

   One should learn from the life of Lord Krishna, who had to face severe losses and challenges throughout his life. However, Yogeshwar Shri Krishna was always in a state of Param-Ananda. He always solved every problem and supported everyone on this planet to establish dharma.

   As per Vedantic philosophy mentioned in the Taittiriya Upanishad, there are five energy layers, also known as *koshas*, or sheaths that surround the soul.

1. Annamaya Kosha: a body fed by food—physical sheath.
2. Pranamaya Kosha: vital energy, breath or life force sheath
3. Manomaya Kosha: one that controls one's heart—mental sheath that represents one's mind, emotions inner world
4. Vijnanamaya Kosha:developing clarity and inner reflection as one learns to detach from one's thoughts, ego, or sense of self. Gaining *para vidya* or the transcendental knowledge about the self and what lies—wisdom sheath.
5. Anandamaya Kosha: state of oneness with divinity.

The Five Koshas or Layers within the Human Body

Annamaya Kosha

Pranamaya Kosha

Manomaya Kosha

Vignanamay Kosha

Anandamaya Kosha

The biggest hindrance in attaining Ananda is the heart, which perpetually creates attachment with things, events, outcomes or people.

When one is intelligent, one still faces challenges attaining Ananda as one believes work and success are supreme and as one achieves more, one becomes more egoistic (ahankara).

What if one faces illness or grief on account of the loss of a dear one?

One can still experience Ananda as heart and soul, as well as body and soul, are separate.

One of the greatest examples is of Rama Krishna Paramhansa, the guru of Swami Vivekananda. Rama Krishna Paramhansa was believed to be one of the sages of India who could speak with the universe, divinity and God directly.

He was diagnosed with throat cancer in 1885, a year before his death. His disciples asked him why he didn't request God that all the pain of cancer be taken away and he be relieved of it. He simply said it's my '*prarabdh*' (the outcome of the *karma* which one needs to go through).

He further said, my body is not my soul. My body may feel the pain, but not my soul. Also, my *buddhi* (mind, mental consciousness) is different from my body and thus my buddhi will not feel the pain.

Hence, even in the worst of environments, surroundings or circumstances, one can practice Ananda as long as one has consciousness of mind.

7 Simple Steps to Achieve Ananda

1. **Cultivate Satiation** whether in money, needs, desires or expectations, practically in everything. Practice *santosham* (satiation).
2. **Maintain Shanti** (Harmony with oneself and with everyone around):

ॐ द्यौः शान्तिरन्तरिक्षँ शान्तिः, पृथ्वी शान्तिराप: शान्तिरोषधयः शान्तिः।
वनस्पतयः शान्तिर्विश्वे देवाः शान्तिर्ब्रह्म शान्तिः, सर्वँ शान्तिः, शान्तिरेव शान्तिः, सा मा शान्तिरेधि॥
ॐ शान्तिः शान्तिः शान्तिः॥

(May peace radiate there in the whole sky as well as in the vast ethereal space everywhere.

May peace reign all over this earth, in water, and all herbs, trees and creepers.

May peace flow over the whole universe.

May peace be in the Supreme Being Brahman.

And may there always exist in all peace and peace alone.

Om Shanti, Shanti, Shanti to us and all beings!)
3. **Go beyond Manas:** In the realm of buddhi—use buddhi when one is frustrated, when one is in among people fighting, when one is unhealthy . . . simply strengthen buddhi. Always one should remember that **buddhi is beyond body and brain.**
4. Jivatma: Get in **touch with the divinity within.**
5. Param-Atma: **Get in touch with Param-Atma,** the cosmic divinity, through Jivatma.
6. **Relinquish Kama** (desires, lust, pleasure and artha)
7. Practice and preach **noble karma** and good dharma.

Ananda is Amrit (elixir of life); if it is attained in one's lifetime, Moksha (salvation) will be attained.

What's the key to happiness? The formula and functioning of the formula of happiness.

For ascetics, the relinquishment of worldly pleasures, worldly environment and worldly materialistic things is easy. But for those who wish to continue to be in this world and still seek happiness, Ananda should be the most sought after goal.

Humans get happiness when they are doing good work, good work with concentration and good work with concentration having a larger purpose behind it.

Unfortunately, doing what one likes to do is not always possible and thus one's endeavour should be to have a 90–10 approach.

90 per cent—what one likes to do, and 10 per cent—what others want one to do. If one can manage this balance in every aspect of life, one will find constant happiness.

Another measure for the same is:

HQ 1 > HQ 0

Where the Happiness Quotient of Year 1 is greater than the Happiness Quotient of last year.

Here, happiness arises from a new skill, making new friends, building new relationships, taking up and conquering new challenges or taking on new responsibilities.

One needs to constantly ask what one has added this year.

To simplify things even further, every human being is simply chasing two objectives:

1. *Financial Quotient*
2. *Happiness Quotient*

To evaluate the first one is rather simple. Everyone should and must evaluate it every year.

Valuation of Possessions as on 31st December _____

HOW MUCH DO I OWN?	HOW MUCH DO I OWE?
✓ Real estate ✓ Gold ✓ Equity ✓ Mutual funds ✓ Insurance ✓ Overseas assets ✓ Overseas bank balances ✓ Jewellery	➤ Home loan principal outstanding ➤ Personal loan principal outstanding ➤ Car loan principal ➤ Credit card outstanding ➤ Any other loan outstanding

Net Worth:

Value of How Much Do I Own (-) How Much Do I Owe

Financial Quotient

In this part, a finite number will be derived easily and it will indicate whether one is progressing financially or not.

Then comes the hard part, the non-financial part.

The chart below may help one with **Happiness Appraisal.** The list is not exhaustive and may vary from person to person.

Happiness Quotient as on 31st December _____

HAPPINESS BOOSTERS	HAPPINESS DIMINISHERS
✓ Learnt new skills ✓ Acquired new friends ✓ Made difference in lives of people ✓ Number of times, proud of work done by self ✓ Handled tough & tricky situations well ✓ Handled people well ✓ Handled emotions well ✓ Gained new insights & knowledge which can be used for welfare of others ✓ Met people who brought new perspective to life & living	X Friends lost this year X Illness acquired this year X Instances of complete hopelessness this year X Instances of dejection this year X Lost self control completely X Lost and compromised on morality X Lost temper and broke loose on near & closest ones X Met negative people X Met cribby people

Choose Your Own Parameters and Be the Judge of Your Own happiness.

Growth in Investments:

Change in Net Worth (-) Additional Investments during the Year (+) Withdrawals of Investment (-) Inflation

What does Happiness Quotient essentially mean?

Happiness Quotient simply means a state of **being**, which one **wants to be in,** not for minutes, not for days, not for years, **but forever**, the state of Ananda.

However, certain thoughts, certain beliefs, certain acts, certain habits, certain events, certain people derail that happiness. A few of these have been captured above in **Diminishers**. For some people, a period of unhappiness lasts a few hours but for a few, it lasts life.

Fortunately, the universe has given everyone the most powerful tool to live happily—the tool of choice, options, alternatives. These choices determine our happiness quotient and thus our quality of life.

To conclude this exercise, plot the outcome of the two charts above in a 2X2 matrix, see where one wants to be and act accordingly.

WELLNESS STARTS WITH FINANCIAL WELL-BEING, COVERS PHYSICAL AND MENTAL WELLNESS AND ENDS IN EMOTIONAL AND SPIRITUAL ABUNDANCE.

'*High Happiness Quotient can supersede any financial race*, while most financial sprinters lose the race of life and happiness.'

When Priya had nothing, she desired all the worldly pleasures. But now, she has everything that the world can provide, yet she is still restless and anxious. She doesn't have peace of mind.

Where is that Ananda, a state of perpetual bliss for her? Her path to salvation, her path to Moksha, to detachment from the world of materialistic things.

Few wise reminiscences have been captured in the last few pages, can these be the answer for Priya's unease? Withdrawn and pensive, Priya kept searching for these answers.

Learning 1: Humans are social beings and the biggest source of joy and grief in one's life is one's human relations. For non-ascetics—householders—focusing on relations, giving them due time and importance, can disproportionately increase the Happiness Quotient.

Learning 2: Parents are those who seek the least but provide the most. They are not cared for but provide constant protection and affection to their children, and stand up for them steadfast like a wall under all circumstances with no conditions attached, whether stormy oceans or sunny skies. Yet, they bear the brunt of mood swings, external conflicts and internal wrath. Serving one's parents is like serving the cosmos, as life will come full circle.

8

Plugging the Leaks

Life Coming Full Circle for Priya

Time waits for no one, and it didn't for Priya either. In the process of fulfiling her dream of getting a comfortable life for herself and her family and then pursuing her entrepreneurial pursuits, Priya missed out on the companionship of a life partner and soon was sixty and single.

When Priya turned sixty, both her brothers and their families came to Delhi. She hosted a huge get-together, inviting everyone who had supported MMD and contributed to the rise of Priya and her venture in the last four decades. She was filled with gratitude for the fame, glory and warmth extended by her immediate and extended family.

The evening was made memorable by impressive performances by artists from her village and the photos, memories and images of her past.

Priya was overwhelmed and couldn't sleep for two nights after the event.

She was thinking, pondering and wondering, 'Am I responsible for what I did, or what I think I have achieved, or was it my luck or the universe or providence that enabled me to do it all?

'Or is it all these people who came two days back who are responsible for me reaching where I stand today?'

As usual, Priya went to her mother, seeking clarity and answers to her questions.

The Last Conversation

She had a lot of grey hair and wisdom now, but her mother's wisdom was always paramount for her.

The mother and the daughter conversed endlessly and poured their hearts out.

Priya's mother said that:

- it's your good deeds of past and present life,
- your noble intentions for everyone and for yourself,
- and your insatiable desire to prosper and do more for yourself and others around you, which have enabled you to reach where you are today, despite hindrances, despite people sabotaging your plans and against all odds.

> WHAT YOU CALL YOUR HARD WORK IS SOMETIMES THE BLESSING OF MILLIONS ENABLING YOU TO BE AT THE RIGHT PLACE AT THE RIGHT TIME.

After saying these profound words, Priya's mother, who was now an octogenarian, started wheezing heavily.

Priya quickly called the family doctor and rushed her mother to the hospital. She rode in the ambulance holding her mother's hands, with both her brothers by her side.

Her mother realized that the end was near and told Priya in a broken voice, removing the ventilator—her final words—'Priya pay it forward, it's time to give back to the ones who have given to you.'

Her mother's head was on Priya's lap and after saying these words, her head fell limply to one side. Priya realized that her mother had left for her heavenly abode.

> YOU MAY IGNORE EVERYONE, BUT NEVER YOUR PARENTS. THEY ARE YOUR SUN AND YOUR MOON AND THEIR ABSENCE CAN CAUSE COMPLETE DARKNESS IN YOUR LIFE.

Tears rolled down the cheeks of the sister and the brothers. The youngest one started crying profusely like a baby.

The family conducted all the rites with full piety and complete dedication, observing all rites and rituals and just praying to fulfil their single wish, 'To provide a place to their mother's soul in Lord Vishnu's heaven, ending her soul's cycle of birth, life, pain, death and rebirth.'

After a month, both the brothers went back to their cities to manage the business and enhance the market capitalization of MMD.

Priya also was performing her daily chores but her mind and heart were frozen at the moment when her mother uttered her final words.

> ACKNOWLEDGE, CHERISH AND BE GRATEFUL TO THE PEOPLE WHO ENABLED YOU TO CLIMB UP OR TO MOVE AHEAD, ELSE THE JOURNEY DOWN WILL BE LONELY AND PAINFUL.

Her mother's words kept echoing in Priya's ears. After a week of restlessness and inaction, Priya decided that she needed to do something about what her mother said.

But now her guiding force, her anchor, her first guru, was not there.

Priya's Journey of Enlightenment

She was unsure who would answer her questions now.

Suddenly, she recollected that her first wisdom on finance, financial planning and investments was given by Gautam and his meaningful words had changed her life forever.

Life was waiting for yet another moment that would bring about a transformation in Priya. At this juncture, she felt from within that she needed the guidance of Gautam once again.

She started looking for Gautam's whereabouts. She checked online and on social media, and she checked his phone numbers, email IDs and contact details. But no luck.

A bewildered Priya encountered multiple thoughts:

'Has he also left this worldly abode to find a place and peace in heaven?

'Is he in some kind of trouble and needs some help?

'Has he renounced the world and become anonymous?'

Various thoughts crossed Priya's mind, but something in her kept pushing her to pursue her search of Gautam.

After months of searching, she received the contact details of someone who was an acquaintance of Gautam.

Priya called promptly and sought the whereabouts of Gautam. The person turned out to be a disciple of Gautam who had now become a sage. Everybody called him Sage Gautam. The disciple mentioned that Sage Gautam had no fixed abode, no belongings and no desire for monetary pleasures or benefits.

The disciple mentioned that Sage Gautam constantly wanders and for three months, stays in the Himalayas in one of the ashrams owned by a disciple. He had nothing that people call worldly possessions and seeks nothing from anyone on this planet.

The disciple further mentioned that he had dedicated his life to the sole purpose of serving humanity and helping everyone reach their spiritual goal. He had renounced

Grihastha Ashram and had taken Sanyasa, giving up all materialistic things and the actions that lead to the acquisition of those materialistic things.

Listening to these words was calming, soothing and reassuring to Priya. It felt like her mother putting her gentle hand around her forehead when she was in pain. Priya was glad that she had finally found her mentor and would be able to connect and converse with him.

Priya expressed her desire to meet Sage Gautam. The disciple said that he generally didn't meet anyone when he was in the Himalayas and suggested that she should wait for him to come down from the mountains. When he was wandering, travelling and preaching about life, living and spirituality, then she could meet him.

Priya was getting impatient and pleaded if she could meet him soon for only half an hour.

The disciple requested Priya to give him some time so he could contact Sage Gautam and seek his permission.

Priya was restless and desirous of meeting her mentor. She was hoping that she would get a new direction in her life, just as she had many years ago.

After a week and a half, suddenly, Priya's phone rang late in the evening. The disciple was on the phone and said that contact with Sage Gautam could be established by another disciple and that Sage Gautam had kindly agreed to meet Priya. The disciple further mentioned that Sage Gautam had requested the disciple to accompany Priya and bring her to his abode—a small hut, where he was presently staying in the Himalayas.

The very next day, Priya left for Rishikesh. After reaching Rishikesh, the duo carried on for another six hours in the Himalayas by road. Finally, Priya and the disciple reached a small village on a hill. Priya and the disciple rested in a guest house for the night.

The disciple suggested that there would be an hour's journey on foot to reach the place and hence, it was ideal to leave early.

The next day, the disciple and Priya reached Sage Gautam's hut, where he was meditating.

After a few minutes, Sage Gautam opened his eyes. His eyes sparkled with pleasure at seeing Priya after so many years.

Priya was delighted and overwhelmed at the same time.

The disciple left Priya and her mentor alone and said that he would come back in the evening to take Priya back.

Sage Gautam offered Priya some *kaadha* (an Ayurvedic drink) that removed all her fatigue.

Sage Gautam asked Priya what made her come to the Himalayas and how he could be of assistance to her.

Priya narrated her entire life story in detail, with all that had happened since the last time he had met her. She also narrated the last words her mother had uttered before she left her. She requested Sage Gautam to give her direction.

Sage Gautam listened to every word Priya spoke patiently, paused for a while, thought about it and said, 'Delve, seek and follow what your mother told you to do and pursue the fourth aspect of Purushartha, the reason why the soul takes human form.'

What is the purpose of life?

Why was human life created on this planet?

How can one lead a meaningful life for the time one has on this earth?

What is Purushartha?

'Purushartha' (पुरुषार्थ) is the only way to seek truth and attain salvation. Purushartha means '**object of human pursuit**'.

There are four Purusharthas:

a. Dharma: The right thing, righteousness.
b. Artha: Money, wealth.
c. Kama: Desire.
d. Moksha: Liberation of soul, unification of soul with Param-Atma, breaking the cycle of birth, life and death.

What is dharma?

Dharma is **the moral law governing individual conduct.** In other words, dharma is the doctrine, the universal truth common to all individuals at all times. The basic principles of cosmic or individual existence—divine law—in simpler terms, righteousness, universal ethics and values.

The question that was being pondered: why do souls take human form?

It's a blessing for a soul to get human life and hence, it should be appropriately used. A soul has to pass through 84 lakh life forms to attain human life.

Three reasons/purposes for attaining human form:

– To attain gyan or knowledge. Gyan or knowledge can't be attained by the soul and it needs a body (medium) to attain gyan, after which one gets enlightenment, and then Moksha, once the karma phal or outcome of all past and present deeds is neutralized or one is completely soaked in nishkaam karma (doing deeds without getting entangled in their outcome).
– To attain Moksha, or for one to end the circle of birth and death, after fulfiling one's unsatiated

desires (kama) which are in line with dharma (Not Dharma Avirudh Kama which contradicts dharma).
  – To benefit every life form on this planet (the question one should constantly ask oneself is, am I useful to someone or something beyond myself?).

For Gyan and Moksha, one needs to live a life of Karmayogis (yoga in action or performing one's duties without worrying about the benefits of such acts and dharma).

For one who pursues and follows the path of dharma is always fearless and is protected. The verse that states that in Sanskrit is:

'धर्मो रक्षति रक्षितः' — Dharma Protects the Protector

What are the levels of dharma?

Is the dharma for a child, for a parent, for a soldier, for a statesman and for a doctor the same? Let's delve deeper.

  a. **Vyakti Dharma:** Swadharama—individual dharma

  I. Samanya Dharma: Common dharma, which each individual should pursue. One of the Samanya Dharma includes Swasthya Dharma—health dharma.

  This is of three kinds:

  i. Physical health
  ii. Mental and emotional health
  iii. Spiritual health
  Health is important, as a healthy mind, a healthy body and a healthy heart energize and enable karma, which can be beneficial for the family, community, society and nation.

One is only the trustee or custodian of one's own body and this body belongs to the family, then to society and then to the nation, as stated above.

II. Vishesh Dharma: Specific to one's profession, virtues and position.

III. Shrestha Dharma: This is also the dharma of leaders—leaders not by position but by virtue. Practicing Shrestha Dharma at any level will aid in attaining a leadership mindset and then leadership itself.

Shrestha Dharma is of two types.

i. Behaviour or *aacharan*—This includes having polite and inspiring language, excellent behaviour with everyone, being punctual, committed, sticking to one's word etc. (ii) **Higher standards** of actions and commitment as compared to other common humans.

b. **Organizational Dharma:** Dharma in relation to every stakeholder—internal and external.
Internal includes shareholders, employees, employees' families, board members, suppliers, vendors, distributors, wholesalers, customers and other stakeholders on whom the impact is direct.
External includes community, society, ecology, nation and Mother Nature.

c. **Raj Dharma:** The best explanation of this has been given in the Ramayana—how one should take care of one's kingdom and one's *praja* (subjects) (As Lord Ram's father, King Dashrath, explained to him about Raj Dharma).

d. **Rashtra (country) Dharma:** This is supreme and supersedes all other dharma. Duty and responsibility to the motherland are foremost and absolute.

e. **Varna Ashram Dharma:** Knowing and then transmitting values to future generations.

f. **Jeeva Ashram Dharma:** Dharma at various stages of life. Brahmacharya (student), Grihastha (householder), Vanaprastha (retired) and Sanyasa (renunciate).

When two dharmas clash, the higher dharma should prevail.

Duryodhana's dilemma (dilemma of an evil man)

दुर्योधन उवाच । — Duryodhan says —
जानामि धर्मं न च मे प्रवृत्ति-
र्जानामि पापं न च मे निवृत्तिः ।
केनापि देवेन हृदि स्थितेन यथा नियुक्तोऽस्मि तथा करोमि

(I know what dharma is, but I cannot abide by it. I know what adharma is, but I cannot restrain myself from it. I will do whatever I feel is right)

> PEOPLE ARE VICTIMS OF THEIR SENSES. WHAT THEY ARE PURSUING IS SOMETIMES WRONG, BUT TURN A BLIND EYE TOWARDS THEIR CONSCIENCE.

Duryodhana was pursuing adharma as he couldn't shed his ego and false sense of pride.

Most people know what the right thing to do is, but they get swayed by their senses and are unable to perform, undertake and do the right thing.

Artha with Dharma

One should pursue artha (money, wealth and material possessions) with dharma so that artha can stay, else artha will come and go away quickly or will bring unhappiness, illness and conflict.

Hence, one should earn in a dharmic way.

And one should spend or invest for wholesome purposes.

Dharma Avirudh Kama

One should pursue desires which are in line with one's dharma so that one and everyone around one also benefit from that kama.

Gradually, one should endeavour to reduce one's desires and use one's time and energy more for spiritual development.

Sage Gautam went on to say, 'Priya, you have achieved kama and artha through dharma and now is the time you should pursue Moksha.

'Focus on spirituality through *japa* (chanting) and through serving others.'

Sage Gautam gave Priya a mantra for continuous japa and suggested that she should now spend her entire time in philanthropy.

Priya finally had clarity and her next steps were becoming clearer to her.

It was afternoon and Sage Gautam offered Priya some fruits. She was hungry and ate quickly.

She was exuberant after the meeting but was curious about how a corporate sage turned into a spiritual sage; she wanted to know more about Sage Gautam's journey.

After multiple requests, Sage Gautam narrated the story of his life's inspiring journey.

Secretly, Priya had decided that after a few years, she would write the biography of Sage Gautam, with his permission.

Time passed quickly and the disciple was at the door. Priya touched the feet of her mentor, guru and guide and left with his blessings.

Reiterating, Recapturing and Reimagining What it Takes For Humans to Succeed

Emotions Influence the Human Mind

Mind is a great servant but a scary master and emotions influence it. Research shows that emotions substantially influence cognitive processes in humans. The way we perceive things and behave in different situations is greatly determined by our emotions.

Imagine if one is asked to lift a 30 kg gas cylinder and walk for half a kilometre. It would be a challenge for a common man with a common physique. But when the same man is asked to lift his girlfriend and walk for a kilometre, he can do it easily.

Similarly, when two friends meet and one lifts the other one, who is one and a half times the other one's weight, with ease, where does that strength come from?

It has to do with emotions.

Emotions are nothing but energy in motion and thus are critical for any action to be undertaken. Emotions also give courage, fearlessness and the nerve to make bold decisions as well as to face tough times.

But emotions with a negative undertone can destroy as well and thus, a correction in the subconscious mind is required.

That can happen through three methods:

1. **Habits**
   Habits are formed through practice, repetition and discipline. They help in reshaping muscle memory.

2. **Affirmations, Re-affirmations and Self Talk**

The mind can't distinguish between real and fake, physical and virtual, original and copy. Hence, even while watching a fictional movie, tears roll down the cheeks when a sad or sentimental scene is playing.

Self-talk and self-conversation give one strength. Research shows that self-talk improves self-esteem, reduces stress and encourages wellbeing.

Affirmations and re-affirmations reprogramme one's belief system. Citing an example from cricket, Sachin Tendulkar became a great batsman at a young age just because he had strong self-belief. Similarly, in the negative context, young boys and girls can be programmed easily to become fearless suicide bombers.

Meditation and Visualization

Meditation and visualization help reduce the flow of thoughts, cleansing the thought process and improving brain strength. On average, about 6,200 thoughts emerge in the human brain daily. Seventy per cent of such thoughts are repetitive and linked with the second primary emotion, fear. Love, which is the first primary emotion, constitutes only 30 per cent of our thoughts.

Fear was good for survival in the initial stages of evolution and thus dominated human thoughts.

All three above can be used for constructive work or destructive work for self and others.

Priya's Next Step, a Step Towards Spirituality

Priya came back to Delhi and pondered everything that her mentor had said.

The very next day, she called both her brothers to Delhi and discussed the succession plan and her plan for the rest of her life.

After the discussions, she convened a special board meeting, giving a month's notice, and shared her plan for the company.

She declared that she had decided to move on from the affairs of the company. Priya further took the bold step of moving her shareholding, which was 30 per cent, in MMD to the Priya MMD Foundation, which would undertake only social initiatives. Priya also decided that she would look after the growth and expansion of MMD Bhojan Vidyalaya. Hari would be the chairman of MMD (the listed entity) and would lead all international initiatives, while Priya's other brother would be appointed CEO, taking over the reins of the company and running the day-to-day operations.

Before ending the meeting, Priya said that the mission of MMD and all its partners, employees, vendors, associates and everyone whose lives MMD touched, should be to have a shared vision of **wholesome prosperity.** She explained that through her last presentation and that remained the foundation of MMD and many other corporate entities in the decades that followed.

After retiring Priya was feeling lighter and better. But one thought constantly crossed her mind, had she gotten married, would it have been possible for her to work hard, remain focused and pursue her dreams?

From her elders and especially her mother, she had learnt that marriage is a relationship that needs to be worked upon and is not a relationship of convenience.

It needs time, dedication and attention, without which it becomes dry, and care and love evaporate from it.

She thought she would write a book capturing her struggles, which had kept her so busy that she ignored multiple requests from her mother to get married. Priya, thus, embarked on a new journey of revisiting her life through writing.

Learning 1: Everyone knows that one has less time on this planet. The unfortunate conundrum is that often, the purpose and pursuit of humans are focused on things that won't last and beyond a point, don't even give pleasure. Despite that, one keeps running after them. When one realizes it, it's often late, too late.

Learning 2: How high one can fly depends on how deep one's roots are. Materialistic consumerism will give joy momentarily, but for a persistent state of bliss, an inner journey is a must.

Learning 3: Most have information, and many have knowledge, but very few pursue the path of wisdom, as detachment from the material world and the senses needs will and discipline, and both are rare.

9

Checklist for Success in Investing, Entrepreneurship, Career, Life and Financial Planning

The Formula to Achieve Prowess in Investing

1. CFOT1 > CFOT0
2. CFO/EBIT > 60%
3. EBT/Total Capital Employed > 12%
4. When to Invest with ~ 100% Probability to Win - Trailing Year CFO/Current Market Cap > 15%

How to Succeed in a Corporate Job: Three Rules

1. **CFO-1 > CFO-0**
   Incremental earnings emanating from SKIN.
   ✓ Skill
   ✓ Knowledge
   ✓ Improved version or self
   ✓ New perspective (new dimensions)
2. **Likeability**
3. **Emotion management through negotiations:** Managing our own and others' emotions, and calming our own and others' emotions, through negotiation.

Achieving Entrepreneurial Success: Two Rules

1. Survive shit.
2. Evaluate ROTI and ROST in parallel.

Achieving Success in Life: One Rule

Give and get, not get and give.

Finally, three rules for life that are imperative for happiness:

1. **Delegate or die**

   Helicopter managers, micromanaging bosses and obsessive control freaks are a set of common creatures found across the various walks of leadership, management and parenting. Not only does the person being micromanaged suffer, but so does the person who is micro-managing, thereby killing creativity, assassinating independent thinking and destroying the decision-making ability of the one being monitored and controlled.

   A sapling can never grow under the shadow of a big tree. The person who tries to control every possible action of another person (maybe a teammate, family member, or acquaintance) eventually ends up doing the same job as the other person with no benefit. It stifles innovation, productivity and trust and ruins any possibility of growth.

   The fundamental rule one should follow is to coach and train people and allow them to think freely and make their own choices.

   This frees up a lot of time and energy to figure out the other pathways to growth as well as testing these new pathways for the future.

2. **Control what is controllable, let go of what is
    uncontrollable**
    Long-term goals are important but it is equally
    important to live in the present moment and focus
    on immediate next steps. Therefore, to achieve long-
    term objectives, one must achieve immediate short-
    term goals and to do so, one must act in a manner
    that leads to the next steps. So, every call you make,
    meeting you attend and message you exchange must
    result in something. In a nutshell, every conversation
    you hold, must lead to the next steps.

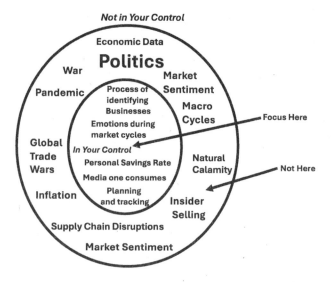

Every endeavour should **move towards or
materialize into the next steps.** When one makes
any effort or any attempt, the outcome can be
either positive or negative. If it is negative, one
should learn from it and try to improve the path,
the direction or the execution. If it is positive, one

should move on to the next steps and execute. **The important** thing here is to let go of failure or a negative outcome.

Negative words from people drain a lot of productive energy, enthusiasm and motivation. If one sees others' words as constructive, then one should utilize them to build something good for themselves, and if not, one should just move on.

Worries, challenges and unsolvable problems for which one can't take any concrete action should be let go. The sooner one starts practising the art of letting go, the sooner one's efficiency, productivity, behavioural quotient (BQ) and emotional quotient (EQ) will rise (it's easier said than done, hence practice and self-talk is the only option).

3. **99/1 principle—paying for peace**
   Italian economist Vilfredo Pareto devised the Pareto 80/20 Rule, and the Pareto Principle can be used in every sphere of life, determining what is important versus what needs to be ignored.[1]

   The 99/1 principle simply states that in life, **1 per cent leakage or pilferage or wastage—** whatever terminology one chooses—will always exist, whether in money, effort, ownership of things or relationships. Ignore it, forget about it and let it go. **One per cent is the price that one needs to pay, one has to pay and one should pay to buy peace.** This is a small price that one can pay to get in a state of bliss and flow whether it pertains to one's work, career or life.

---

[1] https://asana.com/resources/pareto-principle-80-20-rule.

Key Questions about Financial Planning

What should be the right amount to save as a proportion of the total income?

A minimum of 20 per cent of the disposable income post-tax, every year should be channelled into savings. The idea is simple, the amount you save every month should not drastically change your lifestyle, but, at the same time, it should take care of your future needs and uncertainties.

How much should be term life insurance?

- ✓ Life insurance should only be used as an instrument to protect against the loss of income and not as a saving or investment product. Everyone should buy term insurance to protect their family members against the loss of income arising from their untimely death.
- ✓ Since mostly term insurance plans do not give back the paid premium, you can avail yourself of an RoP (return on premium) rider, which allows you to get your premium back in case you survive the insurance term. An RoP rider is a bit more expensive than a vanilla plan.
- ✓ Since young people have a higher chance of dying in an accident than of an ailment, they should also take an accidental rider. By paying a small additional amount, they can double the claim amount.

What should be the period for which term insurance should be taken?

- ✓ Ideally, you should have term insurance as long as you have financial responsibilities. A rule of thumb in this regard is that your policy should expire at the time of your retirement when you do not have any active income that needs to be replaced.

✓ For example, if the sole breadwinner of a family takes an insurance policy at the age of thirty and has two children aged one and three, then they should take term insurance for the next twenty-five years, as both children are expected to settle and start earning by the time they turn twenty-six and twenty-eight, respectively. On the other hand, if one believes that they will be working till sixty years, then, the term of life insurance should not be over thirty years.

What should be the quantum of insurance you should take?

If you are young, single and do not have any major financial responsibility, the sum covered can be three times your annual income. If you are married with children, the sum covered can be five times your annual income. In any case, the term cover should not exceed ten times your annual income unless you have a home loan liability. In this case you can opt for a policy covering the outstanding loan plus at least two years of annual income. Please note that term insurance premium is an expense as it is not expected to come back during your lifetime.

Should medical insurance be taken?

Health insurance is important to cover your unforeseen medical expenses. You should buy a medical cover that gives you protection against major diseases requiring a costly treatment. You can also buy a separate medical insurance policy to cover cancer as its treatment is exorbitantly costly and may consume all your savings. The alternative is to have a separate medical corpus fund for your family, created only for medical purposes. This fund will have investments in index and the amount will be equivalent to the premium you are paying to the medical insurance company otherwise. It is important to note that mostly medical insurance policies have a cooling period of four years, which means you will be able to raise a medical claim only after four years. Also, medical insurance is expensive and, as you age, you end up paying a higher premium amount every year. It is recommended that instead of buying one policy from a single insurer you should buy three or four policies from different insurers. This acts as a hedge against rejection of claims. If one insurer rejects your claim, then one of the others will accept. Also, after a claim yearly premium increases greatly, therefore, if you have multiple policies, only the premium for the policy on which the claim has been raised will increase.

What is the right asset allocation?

- ✓ Debt: You should take a debt only to buy a house so that you can avoid the monthly house rent and get tax benefits.
- ✓ Contingency fund: You should have a safety net to cover your expenses for the next three to thirty-six months in the case of an unforeseen event.
- ✓ Physical gold: You can invest 10 per cent of your total allocation in physical gold.
- ✓ Equities: The balance should be deployed in equities.

How to plan for your retired life?

When you retire, multiply your monthly expenses by thirty-six and create a buffer of 10 per cent on top of that for uncertainties. To reach this corpus, park some money in

FDs or overnight funds to be withdrawn every month. The balance should be invested in equities to reap the benefits of compounding. After thirty-six months, once the amount in overnight funds and FDs is exhausted, pull expenses from the equities, equivalent to next the thirty-six months with a 10 per cent buffer, and allow the rest of the equities to grow. And the cycle continues.

How should you construct an equity portfolio?

- ✓ Always allocate 25 per cent of your money to be invested in equities to Nifty 50, which has an automated system for weeding out non-performing companies and replacing them with high-performing ones.
- ✓ Equity allocation of 25 per cent should be in NASDAQ ETF, which is a composite of US tech businesses and again has an automated system for weeding out poor companies. It protects you against currency and geographical risks by diversifying your portfolio.
- ✓ The remaining 50 per cent should be allocated to mid-caps and small caps. How much you should allocate to each depends on your risk appetite. You can use our 100X formula to identify quality businesses available at low or fair valuations. Invest in fifteen to twenty stocks so that you can easily review their performance annually, if not quarterly or half-yearly.
- ✓ Never invest in penny stocks.

Appendix

Why invest in stocks?

Current situation of investments in India

Most people believe that buying gold, land or property are good investments. Middle-class people especially value gold. However, most people are not successful in their investments due to a lack of financial knowledge. In India, where the education system is focused on science and engineering, there is a lack of financial literacy. In fact, it is surprising that even those who have studied finance are usually averse to equity investing and end up making bad investment decisions.

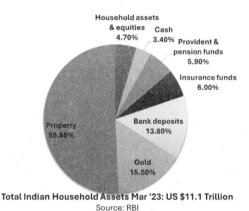

Total Indian Household Assets Mar '23: US $11.1 Trillion
Source: RBI

209

We Indians have believed in creating wealth through gold and real estate, if not these asset classes, the next option every person loves is fixed deposit (FDs), where the capital growth is mistakenly believed to be high. Asset classes such as real estate and gold are physical, our ability to touch and feel them makes us feel secure, whereas FDs are insured by banks upto the first 5 lakh (DICGC[1]). The stock market is a stark contrast to this, as a result people find it risky—a misunderstanding that leads to fewer people investing in it.

But the real asset class which has created wealth in any country is the stock market.

If someone invested Rs 1 lakh in Sensex in 1998, it would have grown at a CAGR of 13.7 per cent to 19.3 lakh over the period of 1998–2022, while other asset classes would have marked lower than 10 per cent CAGR growth in the same period.

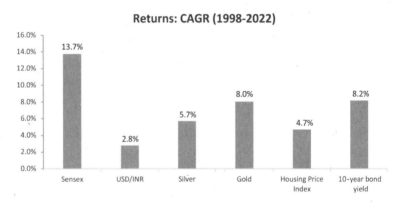

Returns: CAGR (1998-2022)

---

[1] Deposit Insurance and Credit Guarantee Corporation is a specialized division of Reserve Bank of India which is under the jurisdiction of Ministry of Finance. DICGC provides insurance to deposit holders in case the bank goes under upto Rs 5 lakh per person or per pan in India.

'I don't have money to invest.'

I met my college friends after a year, we went to the pizza shop and ordered some veg pizzas and cold drinks. The place was quiet with soft music playing in the background. We all shared college memories and spoke about our current work environments. I learnt that only a few of them invested their money and most of them were trapped in loans with approximately 40 per cent of their salary going for equated monthly instalments (EMI).

Nowadays, normal people don't live life on their own terms, they are always going by society's expectations. They buy homes, cars and expensive phones just to flaunt them in public. The smartest people take decisions wisely and they never buy expensive things to impress someone.

Why does long-term investing work in India?

To earn positive returns from the stock market, the minimum time horizon for investment should be 7 years.

100x strategy—The ultimate power of wealth creation

Shemaroo Entertainment Ltd is engaged in the distribution of content for broadcasting of satellite channels, physical formats, and emerging digital technologies like mobile, internet, broadband, DTH, etc.

Shemaroo Entertainment Ltd's cash flow from operations (CFO) deteriorated between 2012 to 2016.

Shemaroo Entertainment Ltd					
Year	2012	2013	2014	2015	2016
Cash Flow from Operations (Rs Cr)	14.55	–1.07	–19.37	–30.26	–49.45
Entry Year	2017				
Exit Year	2022				
Entry Average Market Cap (Rs Cr)—2017	1,045				
Exit Average Market Cap (Rs Cr)—2022	321				
CAGR (FY17–FY22) (%)	–21				
Absolute Return (%)	–69				

On a conservative basis, we would ideally invest in the average market cap and exit at the average market cap in five years' time.

In 2017, the entry market cap stood at Rs 1,045 crore and the exit market cap stood at Rs 321 crore in 2022. The stock lost its value by around 69 per cent in five years. We should avoid as there being no growth or de-growth in cash flow from operations.

VIP Clothing is engaged in the business of manufacturing, marketing and distribution of men's and women's innerwear and socks under the brand name VIP, Frenchie, Feelings, Leader and Eminence. VIP Clothing Ltd's CFO was there, but cash flow was volatile from 2012 to 2016.

VIP Clothing Ltd					
Year	2012	2013	2014	2015	2016
Cash Flow from Operations (Rs Cr)	22	5	35	12	10
Entry Year	2017				
Exit Year	2022				
Entry Average Market Cap (Rs Cr)—2017	400				
Exit Average Market Cap (Rs Cr)—2022	207				
CAGR (FY17–FY22) (%)	–12				
Absolute Return (%)	–48				

In 2017, the entry market cap stood at Rs 400 crore and the exit market cap stood at Rs 207 crore in 2022. The stock has lost its value by around 48 per cent in five years. We should avoid the stocks if there is any volatility in cash flows. If the company's CFO witnessed degrowth or volatility, investors should avoid the company for investments.

Consistency in Growth (CFOT1 > CFOT0)

Cash flow from operating activities (CFO) represents the amount of cash generated from the core business activities such as manufacturing and selling goods or services. Operating activities include revenue generation, payment of expenses and working capital funding. Generally, CFO is calculated by net income, non-cash items and changes in working capital.

$$\text{CFO} = \text{Net income} + \text{Non-cash items} + \text{changes in working capital}$$

We believe cash generation is more important than revenue generation. The growth in cash generation indicates the company is growing and shows healthy cash flow. According to our formula, the current year's cash flow from operations (CFO1) should be greater than the previous year's cash flow from operations (CFO0). This shows that the company has generated healthy cash flows in comparison to the previous year. This parameter focused on cash flows instead of revenue.

Simply, CFO1 > CFO0 indicates consistency in cash flows.

Indraprastha Gas Limited (IGL) is engaged in city gas distribution in the National Capital Territory of Delhi. IGL also supplies gas to nearby regions of Delhi. IGL is one of the pioneers and leading city gas distribution companies in India, catering to more than 1.1 million CNG vehicles, 1.4 million domestic PNG customers and over 5500 commercial and industrial customers.

IGL's CFO grew steadily between 2007 and 2011, despite the financial crisis in 2008.

Indraprastha Gas Ltd					
Year	2007	2008	2009	2010	2011
Cash Flow from Operations (Rs Cr)	190	204	219	327	410
Entry Year	2012				
Exit Year	2017				
Entry Average Market Cap (Rs Cr)—2012	3,839				
Exit Average Market Cap (Rs Cr)—2027	17,047				
CAGR (FY12–FY17) (%)	35				
Absolute Return (%)	344				

In 2012, the entry market cap was around Rs 3,839 crore and the exit market cap stood around Rs 17,047 crore in 2017. The stock has created a wealth of 344 per cent in five years. The stock has delivered a 35 per cent CAGR return during the period of 2012 to 2017. If the cash flows grow consistently for five years, we should consider investing in the company's stock, however, **CFO1>CFO0** is not the only criterion to invest in the stock market.

Dynamatic Technologies Ltd is engaged in the manufacturing hydraulic gear pumps and automotive turbochargers. The company serves clients across the aerospace, automotive and hydraulic industries. The company has manufacturing facilities in Europe and India serving customers across six continents.

Dynamatic Technologies Ltd's CFO grew well from Rs 13 crore in 2003 to Rs 31 crore in 2007.

Dynamatic Technologies Ltd					
Year	2003	2004	2005	2006	2007
Cash Flow from Operations (Rs Cr)	13	14	21	30	31
Entry Year	2008				
Exit Year	2013				
Entry Average Market Cap (Rs Cr)—2008	504				
Exit Average Market Cap (Rs Cr)—2013	356				
CAGR (FY08–FY13) (%)	–7				
Absolute Return (%)	–29				

The entry market cap in 2008 was around Rs 504 crore and the exit market cap stood around Rs 356 crore in 2013. The stock lost its value by around 29 per cent in five years. CFO growth, therefore, is not the only parameter to invest in stocks. We should also look at efficiency in growth.

Quality of growth (CFO/EBIT > 60 per cent)

Earnings before interest and tax (EBIT) indicates the profitability of the company. EBIT ignores tax burden and capital structures and focuses on the company's ability to generate revenue from operations. EBIT helps identify the companies that are generating revenue to pay off interest or debt obligations and to fund ongoing operations. EBIT can be calculated in two ways:

EBIT = Revenue – Cost of Goods Sold (COGS) – Operating Expenses

EBIT = Net Income or Profit after TAX (PAT) + Interest + Taxes

CFO/EBIT indicates a company's ability to convert the company's profitability into cash profits. The company should convert more than 60 per cent of its operating profit into operating cash flows. More than 60 per cent CFO/EBIT means that the company has converted more than 60 per cent of EBIT into cash. For example, for every rupee of EBIT, cash profit should be more than 60 per cent, this is because it is assumed that 40 per cent of EBIT goes into operating expenses paid out while running the business.

In our experience, we feel some businesses at least need 40 per cent EBIT for their receivables, inventories and payables. This requires businesses to generate a bare minimum of 60 per cent in cash profits.

Indraprastha Gas Ltd's CFO grew strongly from 2007 to 2011, despite the financial crisis in 2008 and its CFO/EBIT was greater than 60 per cent in 2007–11.

Indraprastha Gas Ltd					
Year	2007	2008	2009	2010	2011
Cash Flow from Operations (Rs Cr)	190	204	219	327	410
CFO/EBIT (%)	92	78	84	100	102

Hindalco Industries Ltd is a flagship company of the Aditya Birla Group. The company and its subsidiaries are primarily engaged in the production of aluminium and copper. It is also engaged in the manufacturing of aluminium sheets, extrusion and light gauge products for use in packaging markets like beverage and food, can and foil products, for example.

Hindalco Industries Ltd CFO grew well between 1998– to 2002, despite the dot com crisis in 2002 and CFO/EBIT was greater than 60 per cent in that period.

Hindalco Industries Ltd					
Year	1998	1999	2000	2001	2002
Cash Flow from Operations (Rs Cr)	477	546	661	687	898
CFO/EBIT (%)	73	68	72	66	74
Entry Year	2003				
Exit Year	2008				
Entry Average Market Cap (Rs Cr)—2003	7,353				
Exit Average Market Cap (Rs Cr)—2008	18,254				
CAGR (FY03–FY08) (%)	20				
Absolute Return (%)	148				

In 2003, the entry market cap was around Rs 7353 crore and the exit market cap stood around Rs 18,254 crore in 2008. The stock has created a wealth of 148 per cent in five years. The stock delivered a 20 per cent CAGR return during 2003–08.

Asian Hotels presently owns and operates five-star deluxe hotels such as Hyatt Residency Delhi. The company's CFO grew during 2003–07 and CFO/EBIT was greater than 60 per cent.

Asian Hotels (North) Ltd					
Year	2003	2004	2005	2006	2007
Cash Flow from Operations (Rs Cr)	27	53	80	127	147
CFO/EBIT (%)	161	130	119	120	93
Entry Year	2008				
Exit Year	2013				
Entry Average Market Cap (Rs Cr)—2008	1092				
Exit Average Market Cap (Rs Cr)—2013	246				
CAGR (FY08–FY13) (%)	–26				
Absolute Return (%)	–77				

In 2008, the entry market cap was around Rs 1,098 crore and the exit market cap stood around Rs 246 crore in 2013. The stock has lost its value by around 77 per cent in five years. (CFOT1>CFOT0)—**Consistency in growth and CFO/EBIT>60%-Quality in growth is not the only criterion to invest in stocks.**

Efficiency in growth (EBT/Total Capital Employed >12%)

EBT indicates how much a company earns alone without taxes. EBT is considered operating and non-operating income. EBT is calculated by EBIT minus interest expense. Alternatively, it is calculated as net income plus taxes.

EBT = EBIT – Interest Expense
EBT = Net income + Taxes

Capital employed refers to the capital utilized to generate profits. The capital comprises debt and equity. Total capital employed comprises total debt and equity, which is the sources of funds. Capital employed can be calculated as follows:

Capital Employed = Total Equity + Long-Term Liabilities
Capital Employed = Total Assets – Current Liabilities

Equity is a liability for the company and assets for investors. Equity is attributable to the business owners and shareholders.

Long-term liabilities are also called long-term debt. The company also borrows money from banks or raises money via debt instruments from investors in order to run or expand the business. The company should pay interest for the long-term debt which appears as interest cost in the profit and loss statement.

Our formula suggestes that the company should earn more than 12 per cent of profits for its capital employed for the year.

EBT/Total Capital Employed > 12%

Companies that satisfy all of the above parameters for at least five years should be selected for the portfolio.

Why Should EBT/Total Capital Employed Be Greater than 12 Per Cent?

In India, the long-term inflation rate is around 6 per cent and the long-term growth rate is around 6 per cent. Considering the inflation rate and growth rate, the company should generate a bare minimum level of 12 per cent of earnings before tax (EBT) from its capital employed.

Indraprastha Gas Ltd's CFO rose from 2007 to 2011, despite the financial crisis in 2008. The company's CFO/EBIT is greater than 60 per cent during the period. Also, EBIT/Capital Employed is greater than 12 per cent.

Indraprastha Gas Ltd					
Year	2007	2008	2009	2010	2011
Cash Flow from Operations (Rs Cr)	190	204	219	327	410
CFO/EBIT (%)	92	78	84	100	102
EBT/Total Capital Employed (%)	25	27	26	29	25

Hindalco Industries Ltd's cash flow from operations grew during the period 2007 to 2011 despite of financial crisis in 2008. The company's EBT/capital employed was greater than 12 per cent during the period 2007 to 2011. Also, CFO/EBIT is greater than 60 per cent during the period 2007 to 2011.

Hindalco Industries Ltd					
Year	1998	1999	2000	2001	2002
Cash Flow from Operations (Rs Cr)	477	546	661	687	898
CFO/EBIT (%)	73	68	72	66	74
EBT/Total Capital Employed (%)	17	18	20	19	19

In 2003, the entry market cap was around Rs 7,353 crore and the exit market cap stood around Rs 18,254 crore in 2018. The stock has created a wealth of 148 per cent in five years. The stock delivered a 20 per cent CAGR return during the period of 2003 to 2008.

Cyient is engaged in providing global technology services and solutions specializing in geospatial, engineering design, analytics, network and operations solutions. It is one of the world's top thirty outsourcing companies and operates through eight strategic business units: aerospace and defence; transportation; industrial, energy and natural resources; semiconductor, internet of things and analytics; medical and healthcare sectors; utilities and geospatial services; communications and Design-led-manufacturing.

Cyient CFO grew from 1998 to 2002. The company's EBT/capital employed is greater than 12 per cent during 1998–12. Also, CFO/EBIT was greater than 60 per cent from 1998 to 2002.

Cyient Ltd					
Year	1998	1999	2000	2001	2002
Cash Flow from Operations (Rs Cr)	2	9	12	18	27
CFO/EBIT (%)	77	119	106	103	113

Cyient Ltd					
Year	1998	1999	2000	2001	2002
EBT/Total Capital Employed (%)	20	31	19	22	18
Entry Year	2003				
Exit Year	2008				
Entry Avearge Market Cap—2003	188				
Exit Average Market Cap—2008	1127				
CAGR (FY03–FY08) (%)	43				
Absolute Return (%)	498				

In 2003, the entry market cap was around Rs 188 crore and the exit market cap stood around Rs 1127 crore in 2008. The stock has created a wealth of 498 per cent in five years. The stock delivered a 43 per cent CAGR return from the period of 2003 to 2008.

National Aluminium Company Ltd (NALCO) is a Navratna group 'A' CPSE. NALCO is engaged in the business of manufacturing and selling alumina and aluminium. The company is the lowest-cost producer of metallurgical grade alumina in the world and the lowest-cost producer of bauxite in the world. The Company is operating a 22.75 lakh TPA Alumina Refinery plant located at Damanjodi in Koraput district of Odisha and a 4.60 lakh TPA Aluminium Smelter located at Angul, Odisha.

NALCO's CFO grew and its EBT/Capital employed was greater than 12 per cent between2003 and 2007. CFO/EBIT was also greater than 60 per cent during the same period.

National Aluminium Company Ltd					
Year	2003	2004	2005	2006	2007
Cash Flow from Operations (Rs Cr)	1062	1389	1724	1965	2724
CFO/EBIT (%)	121	118	88	80	74
EBT/Total Capital Employed (%)	16	24	40	41	47
Entry Year	2008				
Exit Year	2013				
Entry Avearge Market Cap—2008	24,241				
Exit Average Market Cap—2013	9382				
CAGR (FY08–FY13) (%)	–17				
Absolute Return (%)	–61				

In 2008, the entry market cap was around Rs 24,241 crore and the exit market cap stood around Rs 9382 crore in 2013. The stock lost its value by around 61 per cent in five years. Consistency in growth (CFOT1 > CFOT0), efficiency in growth (EBT/total capital employed > 12%) and quality of growth (CFO/EBIT > 60%) are able to find good companies. But they don't tell us when to enter the stock. In 2008, Warren Buffet wrote to shareholders, 'Price is what you pay; value is what you get'.[2] The company can be a good company when we enter at a higher valuation, but fail to generate a return to the shareholders. Investing in a big, well-known company can also become a tragedy.

Mphasis a global information technology (IT) solutions provider specializing in providing cloud and cognitive services, applying next-generation technology to help enterprises transform businesses globally.

Mphasis's CFO showed strong growth during the period of 2005 to 2009. The company's EBT/Capital employed was greater than 12 per cent and CFO/EBIT was greater than 60 per cent in the period 2005–09.

Mphasis Ltd					
Year	2005	2006	2007	2008	2009
Cash Flow from Operations (Rs Cr)	161	166	167	379	1,052
CFO/EBIT (%)	142	106	84	66	108
EBT/Total Capital Employed (%)	18	23	20	22	41
Entry Year	2010				
Exit Year	2015				
Entry Average Market Cap (Rs Cr)—2010	13,372				

---

[2] 'Letter to partners, 20 January 1966', in *Warren Buffett Speaks* (2007), available at https://www.oxfordreference.com/display/10.1093/acref/9780191866692.001.0001/q-oro-ed6-00012078.

Mphasis Ltd					
Year	2005	2006	2007	2008	2009
Exit Average Market Cap (Rs Cr)—2015	8648				
CAGR (FY10–FY15) (%)	–8				
Absolute Return (%)	–35				

In 2010, the entry market cap was around Rs 13,372 crore and the exit market cap stood around Rs 8,648 crore in 2015. The stock has lost its value by around 35 per cent in five years.

CG Power and Industrial Solutions is a global enterprise providing end-to-end solutions to utilities, industries and consumers for the management and application of efficient and sustainable electrical energy. It offers products, services and solutions in two main business segments: power systems and industrial systems.

CG Power and Industrial Solutions Ltd					
Year	2006	2007	2008	2009	2010
Cash Flow from Operations (Rs Cr)	196	379	579	944	1,056
CFO/EBIT (%)	62	77	83	100	86
EBT/Total Capital Employed (%)	23	23	29	34	40

CG Power and Industrial Solutions Ltd					
Year	2006	2007	2008	2009	2010
Entry Year	2011				
Exit Year	2016				
Entry Average Market Cap in2011 (Rs cr)	13,525				
Exit Average Market Cap in 2016 (Rs cr)	5,437				
CAGR (FY11–FY16) (%)	–17				
Absolute Return (%)	–60				

The company's EBT/capital employed was greater than 12 per cent and CFO/EBIT was greater than 60 per cent between 2006 and 2010.

In 2011, the entry market cap was around Rs 13,525 crore and the exit market cap stood around Rs 5,437 crore in 2016. The stock has lost its value by around 60 per cent in five years.

Airtel is a global communications solutions provider with over 491 million customers in seventeen countries across South Asia and Africa. The company ranks among the top three mobile operators globally and its networks cover over two billion people. Airtel is India's largest integrated communications solutions provider and the second largest mobile operator in Africa.

Bharti Airtel Ltd					
Year	2006	2007	2008	2009	2010
Cash Flow from Operations (Rs Cr)	4,870	8,466	12,324	13,712	15,456
EBT/Total Capital Employed (%)	19	28	23	20	22
CFO/EBIT (%)	188	170	156	126	144
Entry Year	2011				
Exit Year	2016				
Entry Average Market Cap (Rs Cr)—2011	1,40,460				
Exit Average Market Cap (Rs Cr)—2016	1,33,283				
CAGR (FY11–FY16) (%)	–1				
Absolute Return (%)	–5				

Bharti Airtel Ltd's EBT/capital employed was greater than 12 per cent and the CFO/EBIT was greater than 60 per cent during the period 2006–10.

In 2011, the entry market cap was around Rs 1,40,460 crore, and the exit market cap stood around Rs 1,33,283 crore in 2016. The stock has lost its value by around 5 per cent in five years.

National Aluminium Company Ltd, Mphasis Ltd, CG Power, Industrial solutions Ltd, and Bharti Airtel Ltd have satisfied all the three formulae mentioned earlier, but these companies destroyed investors' wealth in the period mentioned earlier. Those who lost money in these companies during the aforesaid period had invested in these companies at a wrong time when the stocks of these companies were significantly overvalued. So, wrong entry into stocks leads to wealth destruction.

Valuation or price for growth (Trailing Year CFO/ Market Cap > 15%)

Market capitalization indicates the total market value of all outstanding shares. It indicates the size of the company. Market capitalization can be calculated using share price and the number of outstanding shares.

Market Capitalization = Share Price X Number of
Outstanding Shares

The markets may be random and, as a result, we may not be able to time them. Our formula shows the velocity of the cash flows from the business and how fast the business recovers the market cap by cash flows for every one rupee of the market cap. In simpler terms, the investor is paying many times the value for the cash flows the company is generating. How soon, in terms of a number of years, can that accumulated cash flows through the years become equivalent to the market capitalization of the company, at the time when the investor paid to acquire the stocks?

Why CFO/Market capitalization > 15%

If the market cap is Rs 100 and the cash flow from operations is Rs 15 then the business will be able to generate the cash flows equivalent to invested market cap in 6.6 years. This shows the business has the potential to double in 6.6 years. If the business doubles in 6.6 years, the market cap would become Rs 200after 6.6 years, resulting in more than 2X return in approximately seven years.

Indraprastha Gas Ltd					
Year	2007	2008	2009	2010	2011
Cash Flow from Operations (Rs Cr)	190	204	219	327	410
CFO/EBIT (%)	92	78	84	100	102
EBT/Total Capital Employed (%)	25	27	26	29	25
CFO/Market Cap—2012 (%)	23				
Entry Year	2012				
Exit Year	2017				
Entry Average Market Cap (Rs Cr)—2012	3,839				
Exit Average Market Cap (Rs Cr)—2017	17,047				

Indraprastha Gas Ltd					
Year	2007	2008	2009	2010	2011
CAGR FY12–FY17 (%)	35				
Absolute Return (%)	344				

Indraprastha Gas Ltd's Cash Flow from operations (CFO) was strongly grown during the period 2007 to 2011 despite of financial crisis in 2008. The company's EBT/Capital employed is greater than 12% during the period 2007 to 2011. Also, CFO/EBIT is greater than 60% during the period 2007 to 2011. CFO/Market cap was 23% which is above 15% in 2012. Its shows the stock has satisfied all three formulas and is available at lower valuations.

Cyient Ltd					
Year	1998	1999	2000	2001	2002
Cash Flow from Operations (Rs Cr)	2	9	12	18	27
CFO/EBIT	77%	119%	106%	103%	113%
EBT/Total Capital Employed	20%	31%	19%	22%	18%
CFO/Market Cap - 2003	24%				
Entry year	2003				
Exit year	2008				

Cyient Ltd					
Year	1998	1999	2000	2001	2002
Entry Average Market Cap -2003	188				
Exit Average Market Cap -2008	1,127				
CAGR (FY03-FY08)	43%				
Absolute Return (%)	498%				

Cyient Ltd's Cash Flow from operations (CFO) was strongly grown from Rs 2cr to Rs 27cr during the period of 1998 to 2002. The company's EBT/Capital employed is greater than 12% during the period of 1998 to 2002. Also, CFO/EBIT is greater than 60% during the period 1998 to 2002. CFO/Market cap was 24% which is above 15% in 2003. Its shows the stock has satisfied all three formulas and is available at lower valuations.

In 2003, the entry market cap was around Rs 188cr and the exit market cap stood around Rs 1,127cr in 2008. The stock has created a wealth of 498% in 5 years. The stock delivered a 43% CAGR return from the period of 2003 to 2008.

eClerx Services Ltd					
Year	2003	2004	2005	2006	2007
Cash Flow from Operations (Rs Cr)	0.9	4.8	9.9	20.1	35.9
CFO/EBIT (%)	124	143	89	81	90
EBT/Total Capital Employed (%)	90	627	174	193	136
CFO/Market Cap—2008 (%)	23				
Entry Year	2008				
Exit Year	2013				
Entry Average Market Cap— 2008 (Rs cr)	418				
Exit Average Market Cap— 2013 (Rs cr)	2350				
CAGR (FY03–FY08) (%)	41				
Absolute Return (%)	462				

eClerx Services Ltd' CFO grew from Rs 0.9 crore in 2003 to Rs 36 crore in 2007. The company's EBT/capital employed was greater than 12 per cent and CFO/EBIT was greater than 60 per cent during the same period. The CFO/market cap was 23 per cent which is above 15 per cent in 2008.

It shows that the stock satisfied all three formulas and is available at lower valuations.

In 2008, the entry market cap was around Rs 418 crore and the exit market cap stood around Rs 2350 crore in 2013. The stock has created a wealth of 462 per cent in five years. The stock delivered a 41 per cent CAGR return during 2008–13.

The 100X Strategy

In the Indian context, we built a 100x strategy using a simple construct with four quality and straightforward checks for investments to identify twenty high-quality stocks and then leave the portfolio for a five-year period with equal weights and checked the data where the portfolio not only outperformed the benchmark consistently, but also delivered healthy absolute returns and more specifically, it performed extremely well when the broader markets experienced stress.

Before we detail the returns delivered by the 100X portfolio, let's explain the simple investment filters employed/used. To begin with approximately 5000 listed companies in India, we will limit ourselves to the bare minimum market capitalization of Rs 100 crore which is around 1500–2000 companies that filter out the market capitalization ratio. Then, we look for companies that, over the last five years, have grown the cash flow from operations year on year (YoY) consistently alongside generating a profit before tax/capital employed to be greater than 12 per cent—we believe this is a true representation of the return on capital employed (RoCE). We have not considered EBIT, because interest payments are a kind of fixed cost that is already committed and cannot be considered for the RoCE. Also we have quality profit checks which are CFO/

EBIT being greater than 60 per cent for the last five years. But, even with these quality checks we can't create wealth without having a great margin of safety, and for our CFO/ market cap condition that it should be greater than 15 per cent means a payback period of six to seven years.

We rate all the listed companies based on formulas and select the companies for consideration for investments. For example, if the company has grown cash flows over the past five years, we assign a rating of 5 points or if the company's CFO grew over four years we give the company 4 points. If the EBT/total capital employed is above 12 per cent over the past five years, we assign 5 points and if the EBT/Total Capital Employed is above 12 per cent; 4 times over the past 5 years, we assign 4 points. Similarly, if CFO/EBIT was above 60 per cent over the past five years, we assigned 5 points and if CFO/EBIT was above 60 per cent; 4 times over the past five years, we assigned 4 points. Maximum, we get 15 points for three formulas in five years. We gave the most priority to higher rating stocks for the portfolio.

Indraprastha Gas Ltd						
Year	2007	2008	2009	2010	2011	Ratings
Cash Flow from Operations (Rs cr)	190	204	219	327	410	5
CFO/EBIT (%)	92	78	84	100	102	5
EBT/Total Capital Employed (%)	25	27	26	29	25	5

Indraprastha Gas Ltd						
Year	2007	2008	2009	2010	2011	Ratings
Total Ratings	15					
CFO/ Market Cap— 2012 (%)	23					

Indraprastha Ltd's CFO grew from Rs 190 crore in 2007 to Rs 410 crore in 2011. So, we assigned a rating of 5 points. EBT/Total Capital employed was above 12 per cent over the period of 2007 to 2011, so we assigned 5 points and CFO/EBIT was above 60 per cent over the period of 2007 to 2011, so we assigned 5 points. Totally, Indraprastha gas got 15 points rating during the period of 2007 to 2011. The next year which is the entry year, the CFO/Lower market cap was 23 per cent which is above 15 per cent in 2012 which shows the stock is available at a lower valuation and indicates a consideration for investments. The stock has delivered a 35 per cent CAGR in the next five years from 2012 to 2017.

Hero MotoCorp Ltd						
Year	1998	1999	2000	2001	2002	Ratings
Cash Flow from Operations (Rs Cr)	65	157	205	338	654	5
CFO/EBIT (%)	55	88	71	89	94	4

Hero MotoCorp Ltd						
Year	1998	1999	2000	2001	2002	Ratings
EBT/Total Capital Employed (%)	36	45	58	56	88	5
Total Ratings	14					
CFO/Market Cap—2003 (%)	17					

Hero Motocorp Ltd's CFO grew from Rs 65 crore in 1998 to Rs 654 crore in 2002. So, it was assigned a rating of 5 points. EBT/Total Capital employed was above 12% over the period of 1998 to 2002, so we assigned 5 points and CFO/EBIT was above 60% over the period of 1999 to 2002, except 1998. In 1998, CFO/EBIT was 55% which is less than our criteria of 60%. so we assigned 4 points. Totally, Hero Motocorp got 14 points rating during the period of 1998 to 2002. The next year which is the entry year, the CFO/Lower market cap was 17% which is above 15% in 2003 which shows the stock is available at a lower valuation and indicates a consideration for investments. The stock delivered a 23% CAGR in the next five-year period from 2003 to 2008.

Eicher Motors Ltd						
Year	2002	2003	2004	2005	2006	Ratings
Cash Flow from Operations (Rs Cr)	45	64	106	160	–6	4
CFO/EBIT (%)	96	108	128	102	130	5
EBT/Total Capital Employed (%)	18	22	27	46	15	5
Total Ratings	14					
CFO/Market Cap—2007 (%)	21					

Eicher Motors Ltd's CFO grew from Rs 45 crore to Rs 160 crore over the period of 2002 to 2006 and cash flows went negative in 2006. So, we assigned a rating of 4 points. EBT/Total Capital employed was above 12 per cent over the period of 2002 to 2006, so we assigned 5 points and CFO/EBIT was above 60 per cent over the period of 2002 to 2006, so we assigned 5 points. Totally, Eicher Motors got 14 points rating during the period of 2002 to 2006. The next year which is the entry year, the CFO/Lower market cap was 21 per cent which is above 15 per cent in 2007 which shows the stock is available at a lower valuation and indicates a consideration for investments. The stock delivered 41 per cent CAGR in the next five-year period from 2007 to 2012.

HCL Technologies Ltd						
Year	2003	2004	2005	2006	2007	Ratings
Cash Flow from Operations (Rs Cr)	407	434	595	754	1080	5
CFO/EBIT (%)	134	53	82	92	75	4
EBT/Total Capital Employed (%)	13	29	20	26	34	5
Total Ratings	14					
CFO/Market Cap—2007 (%)	19					

HCL Technologies Ltd's CFO grew from Rs 407 crore to Rs 1,080 crore over the period of 2003 to 2007 and cash flows grew consistently. So, we assigned a rating of 5 points. EBT/Total Capital employed was above 12% over the period of 2003 to 2007, so we assigned 5 points and CFO/EBIT was above 60 per cent over the period of 2003 to 2007, except 2004. In 2004, CFO/EBIT stood at 53 per cent which is below our criteria of 60 per cent, so we assigned 4 points. Totally, HCL Technologies got 14 points rating during the period of 2003 to 2007. The next year which is the entry year, the CFO/Lower market cap was 19 per cent which is above 15 per cent in 2008 which shows the stock is available at a lower valuation and indicates a consideration for investments. The stock has delivered a 32 per cent CAGR in the next five-year period from 2007 to 2012.

If all the mentioned formulas are satisfied, the stock can be considered for investments. The formulas are like tables. If any formula is not satisfied, the table won't be sustained.

Portfolios						
Portfolio	Portfolio Return (%)	Sensex Return (%)	Alpha Return (%)	Entry	Exit	Expected Exit
FY03	31.4	10.6	20.8	FY03	FY08	
FY04	28.9	21.5	7.4	FY04	FY09	
FY05	24.3	16.9	7.4	FY05	FY10	
FY06	16.7	2.3	14.4	FY06	FY11	
FY07	13.5	-0.9	14.3	FY07	FY12	
FY08	26.6	17.0	9.6	FY08	FY13	
FY09	46.4	9.5	36.9	FY09	FY14	
FY10	39.3	5.0	34.4	FY10	FY15	
FY11	39.2	11.5	27.7	FY11	FY16	
FY12	42.5	11.9	30.6	FY12	FY17	
FY13	41.7	11.2	30.5	FY13	FY18	
FY14	29.7	8.4	21.2	FY14	FY19	

Portfolios

Portfolio	Portfolio Return (%)	Sensex Return (%)	Alpha Return (%)	Entry	Exit	Expected Exit
FY15	10.6	12.8	-2.3	FY15	FY20	
FY16	21.2	17.0	4.2	FY16	FY21	
FY17	14.1	11.5	2.6	FY17	FY22	
FY18	15.3	13.0	2.3	FY18		FY23
FY19	42.0	12.5	29.4	FY19		FY24
FY20	71.4	11.0	60.4	FY20		FY25
FY21	44.0	23.1	20.9	FY21		FY26
FY22				FY22		FY27

The portfolios has performed well compared to Sensex.

The 100X Portfolio

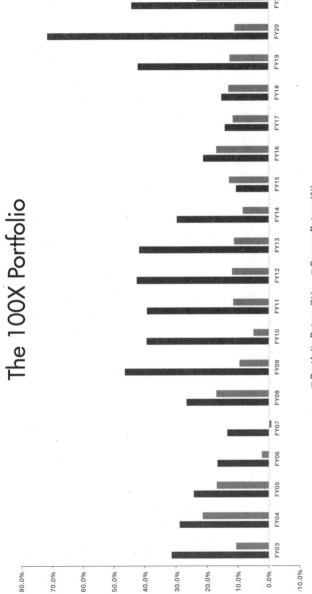

■ Portfolio Return (%)   ■ Sensex Return (%)

Portfolio—2003					
Portfolio Stocks	Market Cap—2003	Market Cap—2008	CAGR (FY03–FY08) (%)	Allocation (%)	Return (%)
Cyient Ltd	188	1127	43	5	2.2
Hero MotoCorp Ltd	5464	15,194	23	5	1.1
Bosch Ltd	2125	12,095	42	5	2.1
GAIL (India) Ltd	9931	32,943	27	5	1.4
Deepak Fertilisers And Petrochemicals Corporation Ltd	233	834	29	5	1.5
Eicher Motors Ltd	264	750	23	5	1.2
Oil & Natural Gas Corporation Ltd	70,434	2,01,018	23	5	1.2
Sanofi India Ltd	889	1903	16	5	0.8
Berger Paints India Ltd	254	1242	37	5	1.9
Bharat Electronics Ltd	2765	8794	26	5	1.3
Carborundum Universal Ltd	143	1130	51	5	2.6

Portfolio—2003					
Portfolio Stocks	Market Cap—2003	Market Cap—2008	CAGR (FY03–FY08) (%)	Allocation (%)	Return (%)
Cummins India Ltd	1482	5653	31	5	1.5
National Aluminium Company Ltd	7262	24,241	27	5	1.4
Samvardhana Motherson International Ltd	499	2923	42	5	2.1
Tata Investment Corporation Ltd	315	1593	38	5	1.9
Torrent Pharmaceuticals Ltd	563	1330	19	5	0.9
Akzo Nobel India Ltd	574	1902	27	5	1.4
Blue Dart Express Ltd	206	1407	47	5	2.3
Container Corporation of India Ltd	2387	10,412	34	5	1.7
Finolex Cables Ltd	342	897	21	5	1.1
Total Portfolio Returns					31.4

Portfolio Stocks	Portfolio—2004				
	Market Cap—2004	Market Cap—2009	CAGR (FY04–FY09) (%)	Allocation (%)	Return (%)
Cyient Ltd	209	1040	38	5	1.9
GAIL (India) Ltd	17,258	38,549	17	5	0.9
Hindalco Industries Ltd	11,134	15,688	7	5	0.4
Bharat Petroleum Corporation Ltd	12,073	16,822	7	5	0.3
Eicher Motors Ltd	486	995	15	5	0.8
Oil & Natural Gas Corporation Ltd	1,09,070	2,14,112	14	5	0.7
Carborundum Universal Ltd	293	1117	31	5	1.5
Tata Investment Corporation Ltd	475	1347	23	5	1.2
Axis Bank Ltd	3290	27,565	53	5	2.6
Blue Dart Express Ltd	453	1192	21	5	1.1
Maharashtra Scooters Ltd	166	152	-2	5	-0.1

	Portfolio—2004				
Portfolio Stocks	Market Cap— 2004	Market Cap— 2009	CAGR (FY04–FY09) (%)	Allocation (%)	Return (%)
National Aluminium Company Ltd	10,581	19,225	13	5	0.6
Schaeffler India Ltd	204	661	27	5	1.3
Bharat Electronics Ltd	4113	10,203	20	5	1.0
Coromandel International Ltd	340	2311	47	5	2.3
Jindal Steel & Power Ltd	1826	39,616	85	5	4.3
NMDC Ltd	5871	1,19,351	83	5	4.1
Siemens Ltd	3405	14,109	33	5	1.6
Tata Power Company Ltd	6426	25,018	31	5	1.6
West Coast Paper Mills Ltd	166	318	14	5	0.7
				Total Portfolio Returns	28.9

| Portfolio—2005 | | | | | |
Portfolio Stocks	Market Cap— 2005	Market Cap— 2010	CAGR (FY05–FY10) (%)	Allocation (%)	Return (%)
GAIL (India) Ltd	19,945	57,437	24	5	1.2
Oil & Natural Gas Corporation Ltd	1,33,679	2,60,332	14	5	0.7
Eicher Motors Ltd	817	2524	25	5	1.3
Hindalco Industries Ltd	12,513	33,995	22	5	1.1
National Aluminium Company Ltd	11,033	26,196	19	5	0.9
Tata Investment Corporation Ltd	932	2439	21	5	1.1
Unichem Laboratories Ltd	734	1668	18	5	0.9
Axis Bank Ltd	6592	52,202	51	5	2.6
BASF India Ltd	595	1906	26	5	1.3
TVS Motor Company Ltd	1938	2737	7	5	0.4
VST Industries Ltd	527	855	10	5	0.5

	Portfolio—2005				
Portfolio Stocks	Market Cap— 2005	Market Cap— 2010	CAGR (FY05–FY10) (%)	Allocation (%)	Return (%)
Deepak Fertilisers and Petrochemicals Corporation Ltd	640	1247	14	5	0.7
Jindal Steel and Power Ltd	3489	62,940	78	5	3.9
Schaeffler India Ltd	412	1145	23	5	1.1
Godfrey Phillips India Ltd	916	1925	16	5	0.8
Heritage Foods Ltd	105	230	17	5	0.8
Maharashtra Scooters Ltd	275	416	9	5	0.4
Tata Steel Ltd	20,885	52,297	20	5	1.0
Tinplate Company of India Ltd	180	568	26	5	1.3
Welspun Corp Ltd	797	5041	45	5	2.2
			Total Portfolio Returns		24.3

	Portfolio—2006				
Portfolio Stocks	Market Cap— 2006	Market Cap— 2011	CAGR (FY05–FY10) (%)	Allocation (%)	Return (%)
GAIL (India) Ltd	22,429	55,694	20	5	1.0
Oil & Natural Gas Corporation Ltd	1,71,586	2,36,316	7	5	0.3
National Aluminium Company Ltd	15,430	20,608	6	5	0.3
Tata Investment Corporation Ltd	1378	2581	13	5	0.7
Bharat Petroleum Corporation Ltd	12,068	22,235	13	5	0.7
Jindal Steel & Power Ltd	5249	56,029	61	5	3.0
Exide Industries Ltd	2308	11,924	39	5	1.9
INEOS Styrolution India Ltd	247	921	30	5	1.5
Seshasayee Paper and Boards Ltd	141	248	12	5	0.6

Portfolio—2006					
Portfolio Stocks	Market Cap—2006	Market Cap—2011	CAGR (FY05–FY10) (%)	Allocation (%)	Return (%)
Shipping Corporation of India Ltd	4302	4403	0	5	0.0
Aarti Industries Ltd	367	383	1	5	0.0
Ambuja Cements Ltd	14,814	21,290	8	5	0.4
Banco Products (India) Ltd	131	520	32	5	1.6
Century Enka Ltd	335	367	2	5	0.1
Grasim Industries Ltd	19,661	21,197	2	5	0.1
Jindal Poly Films Ltd	582	1453	20	5	1.0
Orient Abrasives Ltd	133	369	23	5	1.1
Steel Authority of India Ltd	31,144	54,539	12	5	0.6
Tata Steel Ltd	27,933	50,999	13	5	0.6
Tinplate Company of India Ltd	202	534	21	5	1.1
			Total Portfolio Returns		16.7

Portfolio Stocks	Market Cap— 2007	Market Cap— 2012	CAGR (FY07–FY12) (%)	Allocation (%)	Return (%)
Oil & Natural Gas Corporation Ltd	2,03,710	2,31,968	3	5	0.1
Tata Investment Corporation Ltd	1632	2481	9	5	0.4
The Andhra Sugars Ltd	256	376	8	5	0.4
Cheviot Company Ltd	114	144	5	5	0.2
Eicher Motors Ltd	1016	5682	41	5	2.1
Grasim Industries Ltd	26,599	25,921	–1	5	0.0
Hindalco Industries Ltd	19,844	23,610	4	5	0.2
ACC Ltd	18,373	24,452	6	5	0.3
Aegis Logistics Ltd	262	499	14	5	0.7
Ashiana Housing Ltd	144	316	17	5	0.8
Axis Bank Ltd	20,792	46,130	17	5	0.9

Portfolio—2007

	Portfolio—2007				
Portfolio Stocks	Market Cap— 2007	Market Cap— 2012	CAGR (FY07–FY12) (%)	Allocation (%)	Return (%)
Bharat Petroleum Corporation Ltd	12,485	24,481	14	5	0.7
Hindustan Zinc Ltd	30,604	54,322	12	5	0.6
Jindal Steel & Power Ltd	15,944	42,877	22	5	1.1
Tinplate Company of India Ltd	153	507	27	5	1.4
Maharashtra Scooters Ltd	355	397	2	5	0.1
Natco Pharma Ltd	370	1112	25	5	1.2
Prism Johnson Ltd	1420	2517	12	5	0.6
UNO Minda Ltd	168	295	12	5	0.6
Aarti Industries Ltd	224	569	20	5	1.0
			Total Portfolio Returns		13.5%

Portfolio—2008					
Portfolio Stocks	Market Cap— 2008	Market Cap— 2012	CAGR (FY08–FY13) (%)	Allocation (%)	Return (%)
eClerx Services Ltd	418	2350	41	5	2.1
HCL Technologies Ltd	15,406	61,457	32	5	1.6
Hindustan Zinc Ltd	22,313	51,061	18	5	0.9
Axis Bank Ltd	26,954	58,501	17	5	0.8
Biocon Ltd	3836	6293	10	5	0.5
Pfizer Ltd	1761	3300	13	5	0.7
ACC Ltd	12,090	22,234	13	5	0.6
Ashiana Housing Ltd	148	452	25	5	1.3
FDC Ltd	581	1646	23	5	1.2
VST Industries Ltd	459	2466	40	5	2.0
Bharat Petroleum Corporation Ltd	12,929	26,044	15	5	0.8
Birlasoft Ltd	497	2389	37	5	1.8
Natco Pharma Ltd	229	1719	50	5	2.5

Portfolio—2008

Portfolio Stocks	Market Cap—2008	Market Cap—2012	CAGR (FY08–FY13) (%)	Allocation (%)	Return (%)
Shree Cement Ltd	2714	15,161	41	5	2.1
Tinplate Company of India Ltd	109	439	32	5	1.6
Coforge Ltd	675	1668	20	5	1.0
Indoco Remedies Ltd	303	657	17	5	0.8
Tata Motors Ltd	18,901	86,720	36	5	1.8
Unichem Laboratories Ltd	588	1571	22	5	1.1
Zensar Technologies Ltd	297	1123	30	5	1.5
Total Portfolio					26.6

S. No	Portfolio Stocks	Portfolio—2009				
		Market Cap— 2009	Market Cap— 2014	CAGR (FY09–FY14) (%)	Allocation (%)	Return (%)
1	eClerx Services Ltd	481	3711	50	5	2.5
2	HCL Technologies Ltd	14,587	1,04,948	48	5	2.4
3	Mindtree Ltd	1669	7685	36	5	1.8
4	Aegis Logistics Ltd	223	892	32	5	1.6
5	Coforge Ltd	604	2395	32	5	1.6
6	Natco Pharma Ltd	236	3482	71	5	3.6
7	Shree Cement Ltd	4135	24,085	42	5	2.1
8	V-Guard Industries Ltd	190	2018	60	5	3.0
9	Birlasoft Ltd	458	3247	48	5	2.4
10	Cyient Ltd	1040	4388	33	5	1.7
11	Emami Ltd	2326	12,920	41	5	2.0
12	SKF India Ltd	1195	5206	34	5	1.7

			Portfolio—2009		
S. No	Portfolio Stocks	Market Cap—2009	Market Cap—2014	CAGR (FY09–FY14) (%)	Allocation (%)	Return (%)
13	Tinplate Company of India Ltd	209	672	26	5	1.3
14	Zensar Technologies Ltd	381	2008	39	5	2.0
15	Eicher Motors Ltd	995	23,558	88	5	4.4
16	Ipca Laboratories Ltd	1466	9837	46	5	2.3
17	Ratnamani Metals & Tubes Ltd	328	1687	39	5	1.9
18	Schaeffler India Ltd	661	4073	44	5	2.2
19	TTK Prestige Ltd	215	4162	81	5	4.0
20	Zydus Wellness Ltd	494	2305	36	5	1.8
				Total Portfolio		46.4

Appendix

| Portfolio—2010 | | | | | |
Portfolio Stocks	2010	2015	CAGR (FY10–FY15) (%)	Allocation (%)	Return (%)
Natco Pharma Ltd	584.69	7323.52	66	5	3.3
Shree Cement Ltd	7186.84	38474.32	40	5	2.0
Ultratech Cement Ltd	18247.08	80227.78	34	5	1.7
Zensar Technologies Ltd	695.52	3517.03	38	5	1.9
JK Lakshmi Cement Ltd	805.55	4202.53	39	5	2.0
Sagar Cements Ltd	237.19	649.82	22	5	1.1
Sonata Software Ltd	555.38	1583.40	23	5	1.2
The Ramco Cements Ltd	2651.23	8007.48	25	5	1.2
GFL Ltd	1916.53	7459.45	31	5	1.6
Poly Medicure Ltd	198.04	1961.08	58	5	2.9
Schaeffler India Ltd	1144.53	6828.94	43	5	2.1
SRF Ltd	1576.19	6422.05	32	5	1.6
Amara Raja Batteries Ltd	1540.46	15218.46	58	5	2.9

Portfolio—2010

Portfolio Stocks	2010	2015	CAGR (FY10–FY15) (%)	Allocation (%)	Return (%)
Ashok Leyland Ltd	8584.43	22219.64	21	5	1.0
Eicher Motors Ltd	2523.54	47167.35	80	5	4.0
IFB Industries Ltd	423.84	2083.06	37	5	1.9
Supreme Industries Ltd	1491.56	8221.42	41	5	2.0
Tech Mahindra Ltd	9725.32	56523.36	42	5	2.1
Tinplate Company of India Ltd	567.83	649.81	3	5	0.1
Aarti Industries Ltd	416.97	3359.27	52	5	2.6
				Total Portfolio	39.3

Portfolio—2011					
Portfolio Stocks	2011	2016	CAGR (FY11–FY16) (%)	Allocation (%)	Return (%)
Grasim Industries Ltd	21196.73	39563.05	13	5	0.7
Shree Cement Ltd	6382.66	49065.59	50	5	2.5
The Ramco Cements Ltd	2293.29	12055.81	39	5	2.0
Accelya Solutions India Ltd	141.12	1711.40	65	5	3.2
JK Lakshmi Cement Ltd	550.51	4437.28	52	5	2.6
SRF Ltd	1844.80	8156.30	35	5	1.7
Zensar Technologies Ltd	650.39	4356.04	46	5	2.3
Relaxo Footwears Ltd	367.05	5354.88	71	5	3.5
Sagar Cements Ltd	220.58	1009.68	36	5	1.8
Astral Ltd	371.37	5139.70	69	5	3.5
Biocon Ltd	6851.88	14484.22	16	5	0.8
Century Plyboards (India) Ltd	1372.62	4260.91	25	5	1.3

	Portfolio—2011				
Portfolio Stocks	2011	2016	CAGR (FY11–FY16) (%)	Allocation (%)	Return (%)
Century Textiles & Industries Ltd	2989.88	7556.47	20	5	1.0
IFB Industries Ltd	405.58	1572.52	31	5	1.6
JK Cement Ltd	816.86	4724.90	42	5	2.1
Tanla Platforms Ltd	135.96	387.91	23	5	1.2
Ashiana Housing Ltd	257.41	1525.33	43	5	2.1
GMM Pfaudler Ltd	139.87	512.70	30	5	1.5
MRF Ltd	2857.48	16654.99	42	5	2.1
Sonata Software Ltd	369.56	1648.49	35	5	1.7
			Total Portfolio		39.2

Portfolio—2012					
Portfolio Stocks	2012	2017	CAGR (FY12–FY17) (%)	Allocation (%)	Return (%)
Grasim Industries Ltd	3839.06	17047.38	35	5	1.7
Shree Cement Ltd	16304.29	96406.43	43	5	2.1
The Ramco Cements Ltd	988.12	3830.17	31	5	1.6
Accelya Solutions India Ltd	265.73	2133.07	52	5	2.6
JK Lakshmi Cement Ltd	25920.91	62475.30	19	5	1.0
SRF Ltd	317.81	3079.24	57	5	2.9
Zensar Technologies Ltd	357.69	1351.27	30	5	1.5
Relaxo Footwears Ltd	11063.36	60909.57	41	5	2.0
Sagar Cements Ltd	1316.30	9459.88	48	5	2.4
Astral Ltd	545.97	7506.89	69	5	3.4
Biocon Ltd	1006.38	5091.96	38	5	1.9
Century Plyboards (India) Ltd	128.50	455.98	29	5	1.4

Portfolio—2012					
Portfolio Stocks	2012	2017	CAGR (FY12–FY17) (%)	Allocation (%)	Return (%)
Century Textiles & Industries Ltd	1355.84	6708.66	38	5	1.9
IFB Industries Ltd	4291.50	26828.32	44	5	2.2
JK Cement Ltd	516.74	3827.22	49	5	2.5
Tanla Platforms Ltd	618.24	6038.32	58	5	2.9
Ashiana Housing Ltd	224.37	1873.98	53	5	2.6
GMM Pfaudler Ltd	3004.48	13989.30	36	5	1.8
MRF Ltd	137.15	853.83	44	5	2.2
Sonata Software Ltd	594.19	2661.66	35	5	1.7
				Total Portfolio	42.5

Portfolio—2013					
Portfolio Stocks	2013	2018	CAGR (FY13–FY18) (%)	Allocation (%)	Return (%)
Indraprastha Gas Ltd	3841.15	19455.30	38	5	1.9
Accelya Solutions India Ltd	734.52	1753.35	19	5	1.0
Banco Products (India) Ltd	315.32	1515.07	37	5	1.8
Deepak Fertilisers and Petrochemicals Corporation Ltd	910.52	2483.76	22	5	1.1
Grasim Industries Ltd	25595.55	66859.38	21	5	1.1
SRF Ltd	986.39	11082.58	62	5	3.1
Atul Auto Ltd	221.66	860.38	31	5	1.6
GMM Pfaudler Ltd	116.51	1306.81	62	5	3.1
IFB Industries Ltd	295.21	4679.66	74	5	3.7
Lumax Industries Ltd	323.03	1896.45	42	5	2.1
Time Technoplast Ltd	803.76	3351.23	33	5	1.7

Portfolio—2013					
Portfolio Stocks	2013	2018	CAGR (FY13–FY18) (%)	Allocation (%)	Return (%)
Balaji Amines Ltd	126.14	1842.24	71	5	3.5
Coforge Ltd	1667.53	6534.24	31	5	1.6
IFB Agro Industries Ltd	140.02	610.08	34	5	1.7
Jamna Auto Industries Ltd	281.51	3213.63	63	5	3.1
JK Lakshmi Cement Ltd	1102.29	4145.21	30	5	1.5
MRF Ltd	6001.60	30308.83	38	5	1.9
Mayur Uniquoters Ltd	521.47	1988.72	31	5	1.5
Ratnamani Metals & Tubes Ltd	612.86	4324.94	48	5	2.4
Thomas Cook (India) Ltd	1411.26	9307.99	46	5	2.3
				Total Portfolio	41.7

Portfolio—2014					
Portfolio Stocks	2014	2019	CAGR (FY14–FY19) (%)	Allocation (%)	Return (%)
Indraprastha Gas Ltd	4841.07	23184.20	37	5	1.8
Accelya Solutions India Ltd	10747.50	25088.17	18	5	0.9
Banco Products (India) Ltd	139414.24	170515.80	4	5	0.2
Deepak Fertilisers and Petrochemicals Corporation Ltd	28810.12	52567.88	13	5	0.6
Grasim Industries Ltd	420.14	1953.86	36	5	1.8
SRF Ltd	3046.60	15449.11	38	5	1.9
Atul Auto Ltd	198.26	1206.99	44	5	2.2
GMM Pfaudler Ltd	415.62	2923.27	48	5	2.4
IFB Industries Ltd	119.59	868.97	49	5	2.4
Lumax Industries Ltd	342.57	1141.65	27	5	1.4
Time Technoplast Ltd	531.71	1457.34	22	5	1.1
Balaji Amines Ltd	1686.68	4332.70	21	5	1.0

Portfolio—2014					
Portfolio Stocks	2014	2019	CAGR (FY14–FY19) (%)	Allocation (%)	Return (%)
Coforge Ltd	5793.69	16093.65	23	5	1.1
IFB Agro Industries Ltd	1313.51	7768.79	43	5	2.1
Jamna Auto Industries Ltd	433.54	2293.82	40	5	2.0
JK Lakshmi Cement Ltd	318.33	713.65	18	5	0.9
MRF Ltd	468.96	3593.44	50	5	2.5
Mayur Uniquoters Ltd	177.45	570.14	26	5	1.3
Ratnamani Metals & Tubes Ltd	308545.39	837651.24	22	5	1.1
Thomas Cook (India) Ltd	6205.81	12936.24	16	5	0.8
			Total Portfolio		29.7

| Portfolio—2015 | | | | | |
Portfolio Stocks	2015	2020	CAGR (FY15–FY20) (%)	Allocation (%)	Return (%)
Tata Motors Ltd	127397.29	40077.47	−21	5	−1.0
Oriental Carbon & Chemicals Ltd	523.94	786.51	8	5	0.4
GM Breweries Ltd	343.07	718.72	16	5	0.8
Kirloskar Industries Ltd	569.83	604.32	1	5	0.1
Oil & Natural Gas Corporation Ltd	245633.81	104933.51	−16	5	−0.8
Apollo Tyres Ltd	9248.75	7600.41	−4	5	−0.2
Balkrishna Industries Ltd	6509.42	23767.22	30	5	1.5
Bharat Rasayan Ltd	427.91	3369.61	51	5	2.6
Bharti Airtel Ltd	149629.86	275793.87	13	5	0.7
Bombay Burmah Trading Corporation Ltd	3353.59	7969.93	19	5	0.9
Jamna Auto Industries Ltd	853.32	1534.24	12	5	0.6

Portfolio—2015					
Portfolio Stocks	2015	2020	CAGR (FY15–FY20) (%)	Allocation (%)	Return (%)
Jindal Steel & Power Ltd	10195.00	17680.56	12	5	0.6
Balaji Amines Ltd	362.06	1955.15	40	5	2.0
Grauer & Weil (India) Ltd	428.79	912.93	16	5	0.8
JK Paper Ltd	524.16	1754.57	27	5	1.4
Mayur Uniquoters Ltd	1948.53	1018.12	-12	5	-0.6
Sterling Tools Ltd	235.03	643.27	22	5	1.1
Tata Coffee Ltd	1707.85	1708.22	0	5	0.0
Time Technoplast Ltd	1117.34	930.76	-4	5	-0.2
Vedanta Ltd	45344.69	42826.47	-1	5	-0.1
Total Portfolio					10.6

| Portfolio—2016 | | | | | |
Portfolio Stocks	2016	2021	CAGR (FY16–FY21) (%)	Allocation (%)	Return (%)
Kirloskar Industries Ltd	707.23	1393.14	15	5	0.7
Tata Motors Ltd	128025.52	115040.80	–2	5	–0.1
Oriental Carbon & Chemicals Ltd	619.17	998.80	10	5	0.5
Balkrishna Industries Ltd	7519.56	40626.12	40	5	2.0
Bombay Burmah Trading Corporation Ltd	3162.07	8311.49	21	5	1.1
MRF Ltd	16654.99	34416.32	16	5	0.8
Petronet LNG Ltd	22794.66	34923.48	9	5	0.4
Coforge Ltd	2834.17	24954.29	55	5	2.7
Grauer & Weil (India) Ltd	685.94	1234.42	12	5	0.6
Oil & Natural Gas Corporation Ltd	202513.47	153869.50	–5	5	–0.3
Alkyl Amines Chemicals Ltd	659.02	16342.05	90	5	4.5

| Portfolio—2016 | | | | | |
Portfolio Stocks	2016	2021	CAGR (FY16–FY21) (%)	Allocation (%)	Return (%)
Apollo Tyres Ltd	8797.18	14066.63	10	5	0.5
Bharti Airtel Ltd	133282.71	339082.93	21	5	1.0
Grasim Industries Ltd	39563.05	96941.51	20	5	1.0
JBM Auto Ltd	727.42	2504.04	28	5	1.4
MM Forgings Ltd	532.03	1564.41	24	5	1.2
SRF Ltd	8156.30	48042.16	43	5	2.1
Tata Coffee Ltd	1996.65	3230.11	10	5	0.5
Time Technoplast Ltd	1396.32	1626.77	3	5	0.2
Welspun India Ltd	8413.61	10895.22	5	5	0.3
			Total Portfolio		21.2

| Portfolio—2017 | | | | | |
Portfolio Stocks	2017	2022	CAGR (FY17–FY22) (%)	Allocation (%)	Return (%)
Aarti Drugs Ltd	1323.76	4221.78	26	5	1.3
Coforge Ltd	3181.14	25560.39	52	5	2.6
Tata Motors Ltd	128437.58	148349.98	3	5	0.1
Kirloskar Industries Ltd	1236.46	1409.61	3	5	0.1
MM Forgings Ltd	789.77	1994.40	20	5	1.0
South India Paper Mills Ltd	169.32	221.47	6	5	0.3
Gujarat State Petronet Ltd	10184.53	14890.89	8	5	0.4
Gulshan Polyols Ltd	396.39	1529.15	31	5	1.5
TCPL Packaging Ltd	548.88	705.87	5	5	0.3
Datamatics Global Services Ltd	703.83	1756.04	20	5	1.0
Everest Industries Ltd	517.82	949.64	13	5	0.6
Ganesh Benzoplast Ltd	320.97	712.78	17	5	0.9

Portfolio Stocks	Portfolio—2017				
	2017	2022	CAGR (FY17–FY22) (%)	Allocation (%)	Return (%)
Ganesha Ecosphere Ltd	597.29	1419.59	19	5	0.9
GHCL Ltd	2488.56	5217.20	16	5	0.8
Grasim Industries Ltd	62475.30	103354.26	11	5	0.5
GTPL Hathway Ltd	1688.55	2119.03	5	5	0.2
IRB Infrastructure Developers Ltd	7945.19	13971.05	12	5	0.6
KSE Ltd	389.57	671.50	12	5	0.6
Oil & Natural Gas Corporation Ltd	229920.34	196578.86	–3	5	–0.2
Tata Coffee Ltd	2564.58	3894.80	9	5	0.4
			Total Portfolio		14.1

Portfolio—2018					
Portfolio Stocks	2018	2022	CAGR (FY18–FY22) (%)	Allocation (%)	Return (%)
Fiem Industries Ltd	1024.77	1496.52	10	5	0.5
Apollo Tyres Ltd	14713.92	13040.63	–3	5	–0.1
JTL Infra Ltd	145.23	1354.76	75	5	3.7
Kirloskar Industries Ltd	1124.54	1409.61	6	5	0.3
SJVN Ltd	12071.60	11237.28	–2	5	–0.1
Bharat Petroleum Corporation Ltd	84270.05	75966.37	–3	5	–0.1
Gujarat State Petronet Ltd	10557.63	14890.89	9	5	0.4
Hindustan Petroleum Corporation Ltd	45445.07	37778.88	–5	5	–0.2
Precision Camshafts Ltd	831.49	1248.13	11	5	0.5
Satia Industries Ltd	447.33	1129.77	26	5	1.3

		Portfolio—2018			
Portfolio Stocks	2018	2022	CAGR (FY18–FY22) (%)	Allocation (%)	Return (%)
Selan Exploration Technology Ltd	350.15	269.19	–6	5	–0.3
Tata Motors Ltd	82215.08	148349.98	16	5	0.8
Ceat Ltd	5746.93	4333.65	–7	5	–0.3
DCW Ltd	609.52	1092.36	16	5	0.8
GHCL Ltd	2569.79	5217.20	19	5	1.0
Gulshan Polyols Ltd	310.15	1529.15	49	5	2.5
Indian Metals & Ferro Alloys Ltd	1084.36	1897.59	15	5	0.8
Ion Exchange (India) Ltd	640.85	2682.85	43	5	2.2
IRB Infrastructure Developers Ltd	7064.80	13971.05	19	5	0.9
JK Paper Ltd	2599.40	5006.69	18	5	0.9
				Total Portfolio	15.3

Portfolio Stocks	Portfolio—2019				
	2018	2022	CAGR (FY18–FY22) (%)	Allocation (%)	Return (%)
Fiem Industries Ltd.	568.12	1496.52	38%	5%	1.9%
Deccan Cements Ltd.	517.13	754.32	13%	5%	0.7%
Gujarat State Petronet Ltd.	11041.33	14890.89	10%	5%	0.5%
Dr Agarwals Eye Hospital Ltd.	149.65	344.76	32%	5%	1.6%
Expleo Solutions Ltd.	396.89	1451.26	54%	5%	2.7%
GHCL Ltd.	2198.77	5217.20	33%	5%	1.7%
IG Petrochemicals Ltd.	717.36	2071.67	42%	5%	2.1%
Jamna Auto Industries Ltd.	1953.86	4407.00	31%	5%	1.6%
Sharda Motor Industries Ltd.	721.59	2253.15	46%	5%	2.3%
Sutlej Textiles And Industries Ltd.	546.46	1208.47	30%	5%	1.5%
Ceat Ltd.	4066.41	4333.65	2%	5%	0.1%

| Portfolio—2019 | | | | | |
Portfolio Stocks	2018	2022	CAGR (FY18–FY22) (%)	Allocation (%)	Return (%)
Datamatics Global Services Ltd.	521.67	1756.04	50%	5%	2.5%
Eveready Industries India Ltd.	798.69	2328.15	43%	5%	2.1%
HLE Glascoat Ltd.	146.42	6391.18	252%	5%	12.6%
IIFL Securities Ltd.	977.16	2537.85	37%	5%	1.9%
IIFL Wealth Management Ltd.	10677.01	14031.77	10%	5%	0.5%
Ion Exchange (India) Ltd.	827.47	2682.85	48%	5%	2.4%
JK Paper Ltd.	2293.82	5006.69	30%	5%	1.5%
Lumax Auto Technologies Ltd.	782.21	1251.10	17%	5%	0.8%
Welspun India Ltd.	5458.88	9322.59	20%	5%	1.0%
			Total Portfolio		42.0%

Portfolio—2020					
Portfolio Stocks	2020	2022	CAGR (FY20–FY22) (%)	Allocation (%)	Return (%)
UNO Minda Ltd	8679.16	28017.36	80	5	4.0
Suprajit Engineering Ltd	2339.63	4853.65	44	5	2.2
Century Plyboards (India) Ltd	3381.48	13246.58	98	5	4.9
VRL Logistics Ltd	1643.36	4813.83	71	5	3.6
Datamatics Global Services Ltd	375.75	1756.04	116	5	5.8
Dr Agarwals Eye Hospital Ltd	113.49	344.76	74	5	3.7
eClerx Services Ltd	2124.20	7707.83	90	5	4.5
Fiem Industries Ltd	583.45	1496.52	60	5	3.0
GHCL Ltd	1447.66	5217.20	90	5	4.5
IG Petrochemicals Ltd	682.46	2071.67	74	5	3.7
Allcargo Logistics Ltd	2494.43	7990.03	79	5	3.9

Portfolio—2020

Portfolio Stocks	2020	2022	CAGR (FY20–FY22) (%)	Allocation (%)	Return (%)
Birlasoft Ltd	3464.33	11534.70	82	5	4.1
Cyient Ltd	3953.90	9499.64	55	5	2.8
JK Paper Ltd	1754.57	5006.69	69	5	3.4
Lumax Auto Technologies Ltd	632.99	1251.10	41	5	2.0
West Coast Paper Mills Ltd	1155.50	2101.48	35	5	1.7
APL Apollo Tubes Ltd	5466.72	22993.32	105	5	5.3
Thirumalai Chemicals Ltd	664.11	2548.03	96	5	4.8
Welspun India Ltd	4704.25	9322.59	41	5	2.0
Ultramarine & Pigments Ltd	601.93	978.72	28	5	1.4
Total Portfolio					71.4

| Portfolio—2021 | | | | | |
Portfolio Stocks	2021	2022	CAGR (FY21–FY22) (%)	Allocation (%)	Return (%)
GHCL Ltd	2964.24	5217.20	76	5	3.8
Satia Industries Ltd	904.47	1129.77	25	5	1.2
VRL Logistics Ltd	2719.73	4813.83	77	5	3.8
Exide Industries Ltd	15591.60	13078.73	−16	5	−0.8
Fiem Industries Ltd	1092.19	1496.52	37	5	1.9
Oil & Natural Gas Corporation Ltd	153869.50	196578.86	28	5	1.4
West Coast Paper Mills Ltd	1552.30	2101.48	35	5	1.8
Datamatics Global Services Ltd	1256.17	1756.04	40	5	2.0
Gujarat Narmada Valley Fertilizers & Chemicals Ltd	5510.24	10105.10	83	5	4.2
IG Petrochemicals Ltd	1852.67	2071.67	12	5	0.6
JK Paper Ltd	3214.17	5006.69	56	5	2.8

Portfolio Stocks	2021	2022	CAGR (FY21–FY22) (%)	Allocation (%)	Return (%)
			Portfolio—2021		
Polyplex Corporation Ltd	4140.26	6939.40	68	5	3.4
Vadilal Industries Ltd	699.89	1129.28	61	5	3.1
Bharat Dynamics Ltd	6824.50	11590.14	70	5	3.5
Bharat Electronics Ltd	41179.26	55713.90	35	5	1.8
Mahindra Lifespace Developers Ltd	3264.29	5442.42	67	5	3.3
National Aluminium Company Ltd	14186.61	18460.26	30	5	1.5
Sharda Motor Industries Ltd	1623.44	2253.15	39	5	1.9
Tinplate Company of India Ltd	2405.57	3657.08	52	5	2.6
UPL Ltd	53497.97	56914.09	6	5	0.3
Total Portfolio					44.0

Appendix

Portfolio Stocks	Portfolio—2022				
	2022	2022	CAGR (FY22–FY22) (%)	Allocation (%)	Return (%)
Dr Agarwal's Eye Hospital Ltd	201.68	344.76	71	5	3.5
GHCL Ltd	2964.24	5217.20	76	5	3.8
Pokarna Ltd	1215.17	1892.40	56	5	2.8
Satia Industries Ltd	904.47	1129.77	25	5	1.2
VRL Logistics Ltd	2719.73	4813.83	77	5	3.8
Fiem Industries Ltd	1092.19	1496.52	37	5	1.9
JTL Infra Ltd	720.35	1354.76	88	5	4.4
Oil & Natural Gas Corporation Ltd	153869.50	196578.86	28	5	1.4
Saksoft Ltd	689.32	955.96	39	5	1.9
West Coast Paper Mills Ltd	1552.30	2101.48	35	5	1.8
Datamatics Global Services Ltd	1256.17	1756.04	40	5	2.0

Portfolio Stocks	Portfolio—2022				
	2022	2022	CAGR (FY22–FY22) (%)	Allocation (%)	Return (%)
Gujarat Narmada Valley Fertilizers & Chemicals Ltd	5510.24	10105.10	83	5	4.2
IG Petrochemicals Ltd	1852.67	2071.67	12	5	0.6
JK Paper Ltd	3214.17	5006.69	56	5	2.8
Polyplex Corporation Ltd	4140.26	6939.40	68	5	3.4
Vadilal Industries Ltd	699.89	1129.28	61	5	3.1
Bharat Dynamics Ltd	6824.50	11590.14	70	5	3.5
National Aluminium Company Ltd	14186.61	18460.26	30	5	1.5
Sharda Motor Industries Ltd	1623.44	2253.15	39	5	1.9
Tinplate Company of India Ltd	2405.57	3657.08	52	5	2.6
			Total Portfolio		52.1

Acknowledgements

Our humble obeisance to our guru, mentor and life pathfinder Lord Shiva for enabling us to share our thoughts, wisdom and experiences in the form of this book.

We had the good fortune of having Balasubramanian and Neha Rawat who helped us with the research for the book.

Thanks to E.A. Sundaram and Jeevan Patwa who gave us the idea to devise the formula for investing.

We are grateful to Sudheer Mahajan and Asutosh Mishra for giving us access to research resources and connecting us with experts.

Our sincere thanks to Padma Bhushan Mrityunjay Athreya, the first management guru of Bharat, who introduced us to the various concepts of Sanatan philosophy which also form a part of this book.

Humble gratitude to Krishan Kalra for being a wonderful teacher and Jitender Agarwal for supporting our endeavour.

A special mention to the Narains and Madhavans who, for the last two decades, have been supporting us unstintingly.

Our sincere gratitude to all our past and present employers for allowing us to be entrepreneurial and, most importantly, having faith in us.

Thanks to Tata Power for getting us to do detailed financial planning sessions for their employees and thus, encouraging us to share lessons in financial planning through this book.

Sincere thanks to our families for being our source of motivation and supporting us unconditionally through thick and thin.

Finally, Manish and Saba from Penguin Random House India who worked relentlessly to make our dream a reality.

Scan QR code to access the
Penguin Random House India website